Copyright © 2023 READY, Set, CCMP™ Exam Preparation Guide Supplemental Material
Springboard Consulting, LLC

All rights reserved. No part of this publication may be reproduced, distributed, or transmitted in any form or by any means, including photocopying, recording, or other electronic or mechanical methods, without the prior written permission of the publisher, except in the case of brief quotations embodied in critical reviews and certain other noncommercial uses permitted by copyright law.

For permission requests, write to the publisher at the address below.
Propel Press
Springboard Consulting
3753 Clark Rd.
Bath, MI 48808

www.READYSetCCMP.com

Publisher: Propel Press
ISBN: 9798385836864

Author:
April Callis Birchmeier
Editor:
Emma Callis

This publication includes use of excerpts, figures, and references, with permission from The Standard for Change Management© which is copyrighted material of, and owned by, the Association of Change Management Professionals (ACMP®),
©Copyright 2019, all rights reserved.

This publication is a derivative work of The Standard for Change Management©, which is copyrighted material of and owned by the Association of Change Management Professionals, ©Copyright 2019.

References made throughout this publication to The Standard for Change Management©, CCMP, are acknowledged.

Copyright © 2023 READY, Set, CCMP™, Springboard Consulting, LLC

Table of Contents

PART I: STANDARD FOR CHANGE MANAGEMENT© 1

Disclaimer and Notice 2

Foreword 3

Acknowledgements 4

Introduction 5

1 Scope 5
2 Normative References 5
3 Terms & Definitions 6
    3.1 Adoption 6
    3.2 Benefit 6
    3.3 Change 6
    3.4 Change Impact 6
    3.5 Change Management 6
    3.6 Change Risk 6
    3.7 Change Saturation 6
    3.8 Competency 7
    3.9 Engagement 7
    3.10 Governance 7
    3.11 Outcome 7
    3.12 Readiness 7
    3.13 Resistance 7
    3.14 Sponsor 7
    3.15 Stakeholder 7
    3.16 Sustainability 7
    3.17 Vision 7
4 Concepts 8
    4.1 Change is a Process 8
    4.2 Relationship to Strategic Planning 9
    4.3 Types of Organizational Change 9
    4.4 Relationship to Project Management 10
    4.5 Organizational Change and Individual Change 11
    4.6 Change Management Roles and Responsibilities 11
    4.7 Organizational Alignment and Change Management 12
5 Change Management Process 13
    5.1 Evaluate Change Impact and Organizational Readiness 14
        5.1.1 Define the Change 15
        5.1.2 Determine Why the Change is Required 15

	5.1.3	Develop a Clear Vision for the Future State	16
	5.1.4	Identify Goals, Objectives, and Success Criteria	16
	5.1.5	Identify Sponsors Accountable for the Change	16
	5.1.6	Identify Stakeholders Affected by the Change	17
	5.1.7	Assess the Change Impact	17
	5.1.8	Assess Alignment of the Change with Organizational Strategic Objectives and Performance Measurement	18
	5.1.9	Assess External Factors that May Affect Organizational Change	19
	5.1.10	Assess Organization Culture(s) Related to the Change	19
	5.1.11	Assess Organizational Capacity for Change	20
	5.1.12	Assess Organizational Readiness for Change	20
	5.1.13	Assess Communication Needs, Communication Channels, and Ability to Deliver Key Messages	21
	5.1.14	Assess Learning Capabilities	22
	5.1.15	Conduct Change Risks Assessment	22
5.2	**Formulate the Change Management Strategy**		22
	5.2.1	Develop the Communication Strategy	25
	5.2.2	Develop the Sponsorship Strategy	26
	5.2.3	Develop the Stakeholder Engagement Strategy	27
	5.2.4	Develop the Change Impact and Readiness Strategy	28
	5.2.5	Develop the Learning and Development Strategy	28
	5.2.6	Develop the Measurement and Benefit Realization Strategy	30
	5.2.7	Develop the Sustainability Strategy	31
5.3	**Develop the Change Management Plan**		32
	5.3.1	Develop a Comprehensive Change Management Plan	32
	5.3.2	Integrate Change Management and Project Management Plans	39
	5.3.3	Review and Approve the Change Management Plan in Collaboration with Project Leadership	40
	5.3.4	Develop Feedback Mechanisms to Monitor Performance to Plan	40
5.4	**Execute the Change Management Plan**		40
	5.4.1	Execute, Manage, and Monitor Implementation of the Change Management Plan	41
	5.4.2	Modify the Change Management Plan as Required	47
5.5	**Complete the Change Management Effort**		48
	5.5.1	Evaluate the Outcome Against the Objectives	48
	5.5.2	Design and Conduct Lessons Learned Evaluation and Provide Results to Establish Internal Best Practices	48
	5.5.3	Gain Approval for Completion, Transfer of Ownership, and Release of Resources	50
Appendix A: ACMP Statement of Change Management			**51**
Appendix B: Process Groups Mapped to Subject Groups			**54**
5.1	**Evaluate Change Impact and Organizational Readiness**		55
5.2	**Formulate the Change Management Strategy**		56
5.3	**Develop the Change Management Plan**		57

5.4	Execute the Change Management Plan	58
5.5	Complete the Change Management Effort	59
	Change Initiative Scope	60
	Communication	61
	Leadership/Sponsorship Engagement	61
	Learning and Development	62
	Measurement and Benefit Realization	62
	Resource Management	63
	Risk Management	63
	Stakeholder Management and Engagement	64
	Sustainability	64

PART II: ACMP CHANGE MANAGEMENT CODE OF ETHICS ... 65

Alignment to ACMP's Vision ... 66
I. Purpose of ACMP's Code of Ethics ... 66
II. Alignment of ACMP's Ethics to the Change Management Standard ... 66
III. Scope of Coverage ... 67
- Structure of the Code ... 67
- Mandatory Conduct ... 67

IV. ACMP Ethical Standards ... 67
- 4.1 Duty of Honesty ... 67
  - Honesty in Communications ... 67
  - Honesty in Conduct and Behavior ... 68
- 4.2 Duty of Responsibility ... 68
- 4.3 Duty of Fairness ... 69
- 4.4 Duty of Respect ... 70
- 4.5 Duty of Advancing the Discipline & Supporting Practitioners ... 70

V. Adjudication and Appeals Process ... 71

Part I:
Standard for Change Management©

Disclaimer and Notice

The information in this publication was considered technically sound by the consensus of those who engaged in the development and approval of the document at the time of its creation. Consensus does not necessarily signify unanimous agreement among the participants in the development of this document.

The Association of Change Management Professionals® (ACMP®) Standard for Change Management©, herein referred to as ACMP's Standard, was developed through a voluntary consensus standards development process. This process brings together volunteers and/or seeks out the views of persons who have an interest and knowledge in the topic covered by this publication. Although ACMP administers the process and establishes rules to promote fairness in the development of consensus, it does not write the document, and it does not independently test, evaluate, or verify the accuracy or completeness of any information contained in its standards publications.

ACMP is a nonprofit individual-membership association with no regulatory or licensing enforcement power over its members or anyone else. ACMP has no authority to monitor or enforce compliance with the contents of this document, nor does it undertake to monitor or enforce compliance with the same. ACMP does not list, certify, test, inspect, monitor, or approve any policies, practices, or organizations for compliance with its standards; it merely publishes standards to be used as voluntary guidelines that third parties may or may not choose to adopt, modify, or reject. Any certification or other statement of compliance with any information in this document shall not be attributable to ACMP and is solely the responsibility of the certifier or maker of the statement.

ACMP does not accept or undertake a duty of care to the general public regarding the Standard. ACMP disclaims any and all liability for any personal injury, property, financial damage, or other damages of any nature whatsoever, whether special, direct, indirect, consequential or compensatory, directly or indirectly resulting from the publication, use of, application of, or reliance on this document. ACMP disclaims and makes no guaranty or warranty, expressed or implied, as to the accuracy or completeness of any information published herein and disclaims and makes no warranty that the information in this document will fulfill any person's or entity's particular purposes or needs. ACMP does not undertake to guarantee the performance of any organization or its employees, products, or services by virtue of this standard.

In publishing and making this document available, ACMP is not undertaking to render legal, professional, or other services for or on behalf of any person or entity. Anyone using this document should rely on his or her own independent judgment or, as appropriate, seek the advice of a competent professional in determining the exercise of reasonable care in any given circumstance. Information and other standards on the topic covered by this publication may be available from other sources, which the user may wish to consult for additional views or information not covered by this publication.

Copyright © 2019 Association of Change Management Professionals® (ACMP®) All Rights Reserved

Foreword

In 2014, the Standard for Change Management© was published after a two-year, rigorous process led by an international task force; those original Standards Working Group members are honored on ACMP's website today. As part of their process, the Standards Working Group invited all of ACMP's members to review and comment on drafts. Additionally, ACMP's members were invited to forward those drafts to anyone they knew to get even broader reviews and comments. The approach to developing the Standard was remarkably inclusive. Change Management practitioners know the power of inclusion.

The Standard for Change Management represents debate and perspectives from around the world. Think about the variety of perspectives represented: All industries, for-profit, non-profit, academic, small-to-extremely-large businesses, internal organizational roles, and consultants also expertise from adjacent disciplines, like Project Management, Organizational Development, Leadership Development, Communications, Learning and Human Resources. The two years invested to create the Standard were well worth it.

It's because of this approach that the Standard has credibility. It could have been created by a small group of experts, but it wasn't. Its strength flows from this diverse involvement.

The Standard also does something else: It helps us do our work. In the early days of Change Management, practitioners and leaders would be heard to say, "everyone has their own definition of Change Management." A definition of Change Management was a missing piece in the foundation of the discipline and therefore put into question whether or not the discipline, and certainly the profession, could be seen as legitimate. Having a professional Standard, which was developed in the way this one was, put that argument to rest, removing that barrier to doing our work. At the same time, we recognize that the way we apply the Standard today continues to evolve with the realities of digital transformation, agile development, harnessing of data science, personalization and other disruptive forces. We are committed to supporting change management practitioners in applying the Standard in the context of these and other trends, and our ACMP Strategy 2020-2022 addresses this directly.

> *At the same time, we recognize that the way we apply the Standard today continues to evolve with the realities of digital transformation, agile development, harnessing of data science, personalization and other disruptive forces.*

I personally love the Standard and all it represents. I carry my own dog-eared copy around with me to share when the opportunity comes. No longer do I have to convince anyone that there is a definition. The Standard gives me and my work credibility. I am grateful that ACMP decided years ago to make this a priority.

We've published this Standard online to invite you to use it and to share its content and its story with others. It's for you.

Roxanne M. Brown
ACMP President

Acknowledgements

The Association of Change Management Professionals® (ACMP®) recognizes the efforts of many volunteers and individuals who assisted with the creation and refinement of ACMP's Standard for Change Management©. ACMP volunteers, from the original thought leaders who worked with ACMP's initial Certification Task Force to the current Standards Working Group (SWG), have contributed, debated, and refined ACMP's Standard.

ACMP Board Liaison: Rick Rothermel
SWG Chair: Sumreen Ahmad
SWG Vice-Chair: D. Scott Ross
SWG Technical Editor: Austin Kirkbride
SWG Associate Technical Editor: Debra Noyes

SWG SUBGROUP LEADERS:

Terms and Definitions Group:	Karen Barnett
Evaluating Change Impact and Organizational Readiness Group:	Bill Mullins
Formulating Change Management Strategy Group:	Theresa Moulton
Developing Change Management Plans Group:	Andrea Grossman
Executing Change Management Plans Group:	Mark Bolton
Complete the Change Management Effort Group:	Debra Noyes

SWG MEMBERS:

April Callis	Craig Mills	Terri Ray
Marisue Fasick	Erika Moore	Kirk Luckwald Sievert
Deep Ghatak	Deborah Lynn Morrison	Margaret Thompson
Risto Gladden	Jason Papadopoulos	Greg Voeller
Karin Hazelkorn	Tosha Perkins	

STANDARDS PROJECT CONSULTANTS:

The Communicators, Inc.
Georgia Patrick, *President*
Anna Rubin, *Vice President*
Dr. Rory E. McCorkle, Technical Process Leader

Dr. Manfred Straehle, *Technical Process Leader*
Alexandra Kassidis, *Research Associate*
Jessica Anderson, *Senior Editor*

ACMP STANDARDS SUPPORT TEAM:

Linn J. Wheeling, *Executive Director*
Stephen Cinq-Mars, *Project Director*

Standard for Change Management©

Introduction

ACMP's Standard for Change Management describes the areas of knowledge, established norms, processes, tasks, and skills necessary for change management practitioners to be effective in managing change in their industries and organizations.

ACMP's Standard is designed to benefit both individuals and organizations. Individuals benefit because they can be more effective in driving lasting, positive changes that produce improved business outcomes and because ACMP's Standard enables their career growth through an objective endorsement of their change management skills and abilities. Organizations benefit because they can improve the adoption, effectiveness, and sustainability of their initiatives and because ACMP's Standard provides an objective assessment of skills and abilities to enable more effective hiring, training, and consulting investments related to change management.

ACMP's Standard is a reference for professional knowledge and understanding of change management and provides the basis for the Certified Change Management Professional™ (CCMP®) certification.

The following pages document a generally accepted professional approach to change management activities to provide insight, structure, process, and a standard approach to addressing and driving change.

1   Scope

ACMP's Standard provides guidance for organizational change management. It can be used by any type of organization, including public, private, or community organizations, and for any type of change, regardless of complexity, size, duration, geography, or culture. It is intended to be scalable to the varying range of organizational change management implementations.

This Standard provides high-level descriptions of terms, concepts, and processes that form good practice for managing change in organizations.

2   Normative References

The following referenced documents are indispensable for the application of this document. For dated references, only the edition cited applies. The latest edition of the referenced document (including any amendments) applies for undated references.

- ACMP Statement of Change Management (provided in Appendix A of this Standard)
- ISO 21500:2012(E) Guidance on project management

3 Terms & Definitions

For the purposes of this document, the following terms and definitions apply. Terms and definitions are expanded in further clauses.

3.1 Adoption

Choosing to accept and demonstrate a new way of thinking or behaving. Adoption occurs when stakeholder behavior is consistent with the future state behavior.

3.2 Benefit

The quantitative and qualitative, measurable and non-measurable outcomes resulting from a change.

Benefit Realization
The achievement of the expected outcomes of a change.

3.3 Change

The transition from a current state to a future state.

Current State
The condition at the time the change is initiated.

Future State
The condition at the time when the benefits have been realized.

3.4 Change Impact

How people, process, technology, and the workplace are affected during the transition from the current state to the future state.

3.5 Change Management

The practice of applying a structured approach to the transition of an organization from a current state to a future state to achieve expected benefits.

3.6 Change Risk

An event or condition that, if it occurs, may have an effect on :the change benefits.

3.7 Change Saturation

When the amount of change occurring in an organization is more than can be effectively handled by those affected by the change.

3.8 Competency

The organizational or individual collection of knowledge, skills, and abilities.

3.9 Engagement

Stakeholder involvement and influence in the change process.

3.10 Governance

The decision-making processes, applied by authorized individuals or teams, for approving/rejecting, monitoring, and adjusting activities of a change management plan.

3.11 Outcome

A specific, measurable result or effect of an action or situation.

3.12 Readiness

The preparedness of an organization or its parts to accept, effectively handle, and integrate impending change.

3.13 Resistance

A stakeholder's opposition to a change.

Resistance Management
The process of addressing stakeholders' opposition to a change.

3.14 Sponsor

The individual or group in the organization accountable for the realization of the benefits of a change.

Sponsorship
The process of aligning stakeholders to support and own a change.

3.15 Stakeholder

An individual affected by a change.

3.16 Sustainability

The ability to maintain the future state.

3.17 Vision

The description of the future state.

4 Concepts

For the purposes of this document, the following concepts apply.

4.1 Change is a Process

Change is not a single event, but a transitional process with multiple and varied events supporting the objective of moving an organization and its stakeholders from a current state to a future state.

While responding to a change, there is classically a dip in performance due to an individual's normal reaction to change. The disruption can occur at various times throughout the transitional process before the future state is achieved. In some cases, especially without change management, adoption of the change can fail and old behaviors resume. Stakeholders must begin to behave differently for the change to be adopted.

The following graph is an example and has been adapted from numerous change management thought leadership sources.

Figure 1 – The Effect of Change Management on the Transitional Process

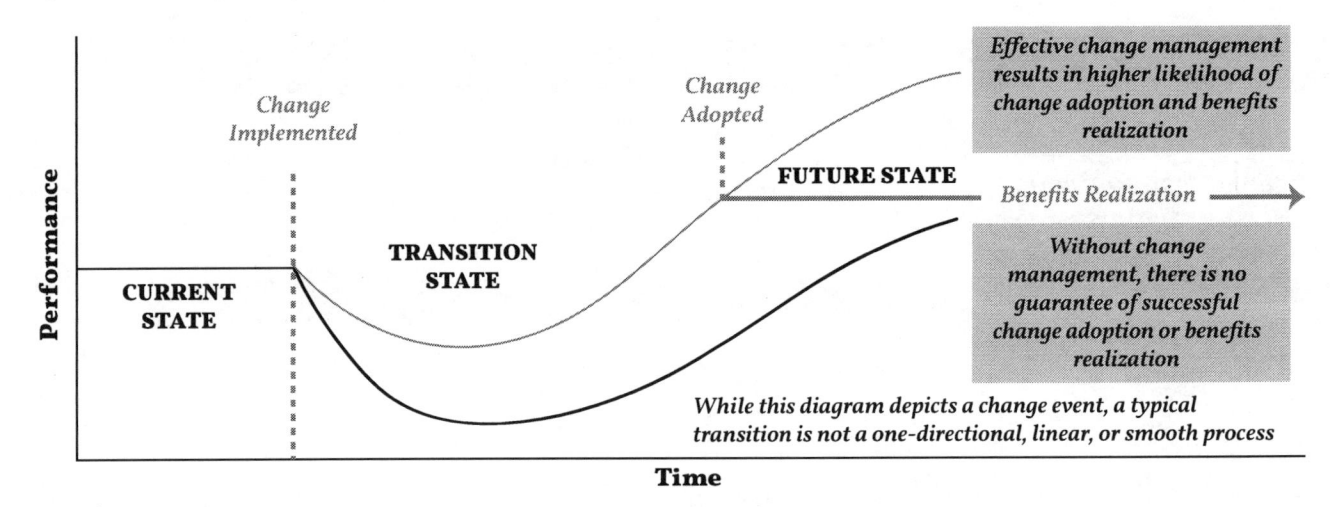

To reduce the disruptive effects inherent to change and to increase the likelihood of achieving the future state, change management can:

- **Increase** organization readiness, flexibility, and adaptability
- **Increase** stakeholder engagement, morale, and preparedness for the new way
- **Minimize** the depth of any performance and productivity decline during change
- **Accelerate** and maximize performance during and following the change
- **Increase** stakeholder utilization of and proficiency in the new way
- **Minimize** the learning curve and speed to adoption of the new way
- **Increase** the likelihood of benefits realization
- **Optimize** long-term sustainability once the future state is achieved

Standard for Change Management©

4.2 Relationship to Strategic Planning

Change is initiated at many levels, yet a critical, natural link exists between strategic planning processes and change management. Strategic planning establishes a vision, and its component activities determine the future state and ongoing organizational changes required to successfully operationalize and sustain it. Change management drives individual and collective adoption, thus ensuring achievement of expected benefits and return on investment.

The vision, a leading component of strategic planning, is an aspirational and future-focused statement that typically describes why the change is needed and what the future state will be like and sometimes includes the risks to the organization if the change is not successful.

The vision statement creates the initial and foundational link between strategic planning and change management because it:

- Provides clarity of direction and focus for the organization and stakeholders
- Identifies high-level results and expected benefits to be achieved
- Sets the stage for leaders to align stakeholders to a common plan
- Acts as a guide for decision making, communications, and engagement

Successful changes require leaders to articulate a consistent, achievable, inspiring, and easily understood vision that guides the organization to measurable achievement of expected benefits.

4.3 Types of Organizational Change

Types of organizational change and change definitions are almost infinite. Defining a change by the name of a project, a new systems initiative, process redesign, acquisition, policy, or procedure update is often incomplete. A change definition must be based on an analysis of a number of change variables that can differ from one change to the next, including technological complexity, number and type of impacted stakeholder groups, degree of process change, amount of structural adjustment, physical relocations, benefit or compensation impacts, workforce adjustments, speed of implementation, degree of job role change, and geographic dispersion. However, what makes each change truly unique is that it affects individuals and organizations with unique value systems, cultural norms, histories, experiences with past changes, leadership styles, and levels of competency in managing change.

Two components comprise the basis of a change definition and risk assessment that leads to the appropriate scaling of change management effort, time, and resources: an analysis of change variables providing insight on its size and complexity and an assessment of the organization delivering insight regarding culture and readiness. All changes within an organization, not only large disruptive project changes with approved funding, dedicated resources, and project charters driven by strategic planning, can be assessed on these two components. Small changes with minimal impacts that do not flow through normal project governance processes and everything in between can be assessed on these components as well.

Change management is not a one-size-fits-all approach and can be scaled to fit any organizational change.

Copyright © 2019 Association of Change Management Professionals® (ACMP®) All Rights Reserved

4.4 Relationship to Project Management

Project management and change management are complementary yet distinct disciplines that may overlap during change delivery, and are often interdependent when delivering value to the organization. The degree of overlap and interdependency can vary between organizations, depending on factors such as organizational structure, type of change, methodologies utilized, competency, and capability maturity.

Effective integration of project management and change management is required to ensure that organizational objectives are achieved. Integration can occur across various dimensions, including:

- **Roles and Responsibilities:**
  Project management should focus primarily on the application of skills, tools, and techniques to activities required to deliver planned change (e.g., new systems, new processes, new resources) in a structured way within the required scope, time, cost, and quality parameters. Change management should focus primarily on the application of skills, tools, and techniques to activities required to implement and sustain the delivered change, such as influencing individual behavior and organizational culture, facilitating new ways of working, tracking and enabling benefits realization, and providing input for future change initiatives. The scope and focus of the two disciplines should be clearly defined early in the planning process. Overlaps and interdependencies should be identified and documented, including how the disciplines will work together, how information will be shared, and how decisions will be made.

- **Methodology and Plan:**
  Project management and change management methodologies differ in focus. Project management methodologies typically emphasize the organization and management of resources and activities required to complete projects (deliver the change) within the defined scope, budget, timeline, and quality standards. Change management methodologies typically emphasize the people side of change and the activities required to prepare the organization for the delivered change, facilitate the transition from the old way of working to the future state, and embed the change as the new norm. The two approaches should be integrated to ensure that the right amount of attention is given to both the technical (delivery) and people (implementation) side of change.

  Projects have specific start and end dates, but change management activities frequently continue long after the change is delivered and the project is closed. Nevertheless, project management and change management plans should be integrated into an overall plan because project milestones and change management activities may trigger one another.

- **Tools and Resources:**
  Practitioners use a variety of tools to deliver, implement, control, and measure change. Some tools are specific to project management or change management, but some, such as a Stakeholder Analysis, may be common to both. Where commonalities exist, tools should be integrated to increase efficiency and collaboration between the two disciplines. There may also be opportunities to integrate or share resources (e.g., people, hardware, software, facilities, finances), depending on the degree of overlap and interdependency between project management and change management.

Standard for Change Management©

- **Objectives and Outcomes:**
  The common objective of project management and change management is to add value to the organization. Each discipline uniquely contributes to the realization of benefits. Project management delivers the planned change, and change management ensures that the delivered change is implemented and adopted to enable the realization of the expected benefits.

- **Risks**
  Both project management and change management recognize that risks can have a significant impact on the organization's ability to deliver and implement change. Change management focuses on risks to the adoption of the change, threats to the realization of the expected benefits, and threats to ing the change. Change management also has an interest in project-related risks, such as those affecting timeline, scope, budget, and benefits realization.

4.5 Organizational Change and Individual Change

Change is managed at both the organizational and individual levels. Change management facilitates the transition of organizations and their stakeholders to sustain the future state. Individual behavior change is essential to achieve this objective and the organization's return on investment. It is also important to identify measures of accountability to ensure change is successful at both the organizational and individual levels.

At an organizational level, change management efforts assess and understand an organization's:

- Current cultural attributes, which may provide a solid basis for or be an impediment to the change
- Prioritization of change initiatives in an effort to monitor change fatigue and saturation, as well as build change agility
- Shared vision and strategic intent for the change
- New or modified business processes, systems, policies, behaviors, rewards, performance indicators, and procedures needed to successfully work in the future state
- Structure and individual roles needed to support and reinforce the change effort

At an individual level, change management efforts address and manage an individual's:

- Unique perspectives, biases, motivations, behaviors, mindset, resistance, and reactions to increase acceptance and commitment in a more productive and resilient way
- Willingness, ability, knowledge, skills, and time capacity necessary to transition to the future state
- Sponsorship and active leadership needs to ensure successful change and coach an individual through personal transition

4.6 Change Management Roles and Responsibilities

A particular change effort may involve individuals specifically selected to advise the project team on potential change risks, such as an advisory committee. The change management team may engage additional individuals or groups (outside the change team) to help assess change effects; prioritize change management tasks; provide feedback on the change management strategy, plan, and tactics; and execute and support the change process at the stakeholder level.

Copyright © 2019 Association of Change Management Professionals® (ACMP®) All Rights Reserved

The following roles are defined for dedicated change professionals:
- **Change Management Practitioner:** An individual responsible for coordinating, applying, and tracking change management tools or activities. This individual is not responsible or accountable for the change strategy.
- **Change Management Team:** A group of individuals who work together facilitating change management activities to design, analyze, develop, and enable the organization to own and effectively drive adoption, usage, and proficiency. Team members ensure activities are completed, feedback is gathered, training is conducted, and communications are delivered in various formats.
- **Change Management Lead:** The individual accountable and responsible for the change strategy who assesses the change, outlines a change plan, and implements change management. This individual has direct day-to-day control over the change management team, the change project schedule, associated budgets, and resources. The Change Management Lead is the primary liaison to the change sponsor, project manager, leadership, overall project team, and stakeholders.

Change roles may have different names associated with the role, depending on the organization. Additional or consolidated roles may be required based upon the complexity of the goals set for the change.

The following roles are created to support stakeholders' results:
- **Sponsor:** The individual or group in the organization accountable for the realization of the benefits of a change. The sponsor defines and champions the overall change goals, scope, and definition of success. This individual or group influences peers and other senior leaders to gain support and provide leadership to achieve the stated vision. This role has ultimate decision-making and funding authority and provides constant visibility to the change effort.
- **Change Agents:** Functional or social leaders, middle management, and subject matter experts from different areas in the organization who are trusted by colleagues, stakeholders, and executives for their insight into and understanding of the organization. These individuals may be selected for their (informal, non-hierarchical) network and influence (without authority) over other individuals or groups. They model the required behaviors in their areas, provide feedback on change activities, and actively engage with others around change activities.

4.7 Organizational Alignment and Change Management

Alignment is an important element of successful change initiatives. Leaders must have clarity of purpose and focus to align people, processes, systems, and structures in times of change. They must also develop contingency plans to detect and remediate alignment issues that may occur before, during, or after change occurs. Change capacity and capability can vary greatly from one organization to another, but the likelihood of the successful implementation and adoption of change is increased when the organization's structure, processes, and people are continually aligned to a common vision.

Organizational culture is another important element of organizational alignment that can influence change strategy success; therefore, it is important that leaders create an environment where followers have the necessary time and space to engage in and become comfortable with the new ways of working.

5 Change Management Process

A process is a set of interrelated actions and activities performed to achieve a specific product, result, or outcome. When properly applied, the change management process increases the likelihood that individuals and organizations effectively transition to a future state to achieve expected benefits.

Individuals and stakeholders need information, leadership support, training, coaching, rewards, reinforcement, and time to decide whether to engage in change and to what degree.

The transition from the current to a future state is achieved by applying change management processes so that stakeholders are engaged before, during, and after the change process. Effective change management results when the perceived negative impacts and risks of the change are minimized and the overall expected benefits are achieved, ideally within the budget and schedule.

Process groups are associations of similar or related processes that serve as guides for the application of change management knowledge, skills, and abilities during change management implementation. These groups are linked in that the output or result of one process becomes the input of another process. Processes within each group are iterative, sometimes simultaneous, and may be applied multiple times throughout the change management effort.

Change initiatives may employ various approaches (e.g., waterfall, agile). Change management processes, given their iterative and sometimes simultaneous nature, should be properly adapted for effectiveness, regardless of the project management methodology employed.

The process of change management described in this document draws on many existing change management methodologies and identifies generally accepted practices rather than replicating a particular methodology. Practitioners using a particular methodology will find commonalities and perhaps additional suggestions for extending their change management efforts.

As an emerging discipline, the ACMP Standard does not mandate particular activities or process steps. Consequently, those familiar with the language of standards will not be surprised at the absence of the word "shall" in describing the processes. Instead, the language describes generally accepted practice; therefore, processes, their sub-processes, and actions are generally used but not required.

The following process groups are used to organize and elaborate on the processes performed by change management practitioners during the change initiative.

Standard for Change Management©

Change Management Process Groups	
5.1 Evaluate Change Impact and Organizational Readiness	The processes in this group are designed to assess, evaluate, and anticipate an organization and its stakeholders' readiness, ability, and capacity to undergo a transition from the current state to a future state. The processes also include an assessment of the change and the impact the change will have on the individual and organization. History, culture, and value systems play key roles in these evaluations. The results provide change practitioners with information to calibrate leader expectations and to scale and customize change management plans and activities.
5.2 Formulate the Change Management Strategy	The processes in this group are designed to develop the high-level approach for change management with sponsors, change leaders, content developers, program managers, customers, and others on the project. This approach includes governance, risks, resources, budget, and reporting. The change strategy will incorporate, integrate, and align change management plans, activities, tasks, and milestones into the other activities and operations of an organization and its stakeholders at the onset of a change (timing and sequence). Stakeholder engagement is included in this process group.
5.3 Develop the Change Management Plan	The processes in this group employ specific change management methodologies and tools to develop detailed plans for implementing the change management strategy. These plans include communications, sponsorship, stakeholder engagement, learning and development, risk management, and measurement and benefits realization. Ongoing integration with project management is included in this process group.
5.4 Execute the Change Management Plan	The processes in this group focus on the implementation of work/actions in the detailed change management plans. The work in this area is required to achieve the expected benefits of the change management implementation.
5.5 Complete the Change Management Effort	The processes in this group reinforce the work in the change management plans, determine the effectiveness of the work, monitor progress, and transition the change initiative to the business. These processes include measuring results and comparing to the expected benefits or business objectives. These processes also include the continuous improvement activities that come from the post-project analysis and lessons learned.

In the following sections of ACMP's Standard, Input / Output tables are included in the descriptions of the change management processes. These tables communicate the process, documentation, or information required to complete the process step, and what process, documentation, or information is an outcome of the process. The inputs and outputs listed in these tables are not meant to be exhaustive, but rather indicate commonly accepted inputs and outputs. The inputs and outputs do not have a one- to-one relationship with each other.

5.1 Evaluate Change Impact and Organizational Readiness

The purpose of **Evaluate Change Impact and Organizational Readiness** is to:
- Review the overall change and how it will impact the organization
- Establish whether the organization is ready and able to adopt the proposed change

Copyright © 2019 Association of Change Management Professionals® (ACMP®) All Rights Reserved

This comprehensive evaluation involves a series of processes. Each process outlines the purpose of the activity, main areas of focus, and key inputs and outputs. These processes are closely linked to the order in which they are typically performed.

The following list outlines the goals of the evaluation processes with respect to change effects and organizational readiness:

1. Define the change and why it must occur.
2. Develop and communicate a clear vision of the future state.
3. Determine the key stakeholders involved and who will be affected by the change.
4. Assess the organization's culture, capacity, and readiness for change.
5. Assess whether change leaders understand and are committed to a change program.
6. Assess the risks and likelihood of success to identify potential actions that promote progress toward change.

The evaluation of effects and readiness for change should begin before formulating change management strategies and plans. Each process output should be the product of wide and proactive consultation to close the gap between the strategic intent and formation of strategies and plans that will achieve the expected benefits.

5.1.1 Define the Change

The purpose of **Define the Change** is to discern and specify the change the organization intends to adopt to meet a strategic objective. Fundamental questions around the change, the purpose, who will be impacted and how, and alignment of the change with organizational goals and needs are key to defining the change. Questions may include:

- Will the change be departmental or enterprise-wide?
- Will the change be people-, process-, or technology-oriented?
- Is the change part of or in conjunction with other changes happening in the organization?
- Will the change be considered transformational or incremental?
- How will the organization and its structure be affected by the change?

A clearly defined change is needed to determine the approach necessary to implement the change successfully.

Inputs	Outputs
- Business Case - Research - Charter - Strategic Plan - Success Measures	- Change Definition - Charter

5.1.2 Determine Why the Change is Required

The purpose of **Determine Why the Change is Required** is to explain the current opportunity, risks or consequences, and benefits.

This process develops the Case for Change to support the organization's vision and clearly articulate its expected benefits to the organization. It should include a clear description of the consequences of not changing. It may identify risks associated with a lack of commitment or resistance if the change lacks a compelling reason and is considered unnecessary by stakeholders. A misunderstood or incomplete change rationale may be one of the biggest risks in successfully gaining stakeholder adoption.

Inputs	Outputs
▸ Business Case ▸ Change Definition ▸ Charter ▸ Strategic Plan ▸ Success Measures	▸ Business Case ▸ Charter

5.1.3 Develop a Clear Vision for the Future State

The purpose of **Develop a Clear Vision of the Future State** is to facilitate the development of the organization's operating state after the change has been adopted.

This process focuses on developing and describing a common direction for the future state so that stakeholders can envision it in operation and foresee the value of the future state.

Inputs	Outputs
▸ Organization Vision, Mission, Values ▸ Business Case ▸ Change Definition ▸ Strategic Plan	▸ Vision Statement

5.1.4 Identify Goals, Objectives, and Success Criteria

The purpose of **Identify Goals, Objectives, and Success Criteria** is to provide tangible, concrete, measurable, and manageable goals that represent planned progress toward the adoption of the future state.

This process directs focus to actual change results and anticipated outcomes rather than tracking the change process. It should establish key change objectives and goals that define progress toward the change. The process should also describe the key parameters that measure when goals and objectives are attained, which will enable the associated success criteria to be identified.

Inputs	Outputs
▸ Business Case ▸ Charter ▸ Strategic Plan ▸ Vision Statement ▸ Change Definition	▸ Change Objectives and Goals ▸ Success Criteria and Measures

5.1.5 Identify Sponsors Accountable for the Change

The purpose of **Identify Sponsors Accountable for the Change** is to connect the change to its owners and determine accountability requirements.

This process identifies the sponsors accountable for the change and assesses their alignment with and commitment to the change. It may involve completing a role analysis to differentiate accountable individuals and groups from those who are responsible. Those accountable are required to bring the change to completion, whereas those responsible are operationally required to do the day-to-day work of driving the change to achieve its goals and objectives.

As in **5.1.6 Identify Stakeholders Affected by the Change**, this process should capture information related to motivations, abilities, expectations, and concerns regarding the change. This information can be captured through a variety of methods, such as structured interviews and general discussions to identify potential constraints, conflicts, or concerns.

Inputs	Outputs
▸ Change Definition ▸ Charter ▸ Stakeholder Analysis ▸ Current Organizational Charts and Profiles	▸ Sponsor Identification ▸ Sponsor Assessment

5.1.6 Identify Stakeholders Affected by the Change

The purpose of **Identify Stakeholders Affected by the Change** is to identify stakeholder attributes, such as level of influence, commitment, or rules, and determine the size, scope, and complexity of the change's impact on key individuals and groups.

This process identifies those affected by the change and those with the ability to influence the outcome. The process also establishes roles within the change initiative and may identify individuals or groups with multiple roles. The process should group stakeholders to facilitate organizational and individual change activities.

A comprehensive Stakeholder Analysis is used in the development of the Change Management Strategy. It is also used to prepare stakeholder engagement, communication, and learning development plans.

This process should capture information regarding motivations, expectations, concerns, and attitudes toward the change. The information can be captured through a variety of methods, such as structured interviews, general discussions, and questionnaires.

Inputs	Outputs
▸ Change Definition ▸ Vision Statement ▸ Current Organizational Charts and Profiles ▸ Research ▸ Charter	▸ Stakeholder Analysis

5.1.7 Assess the Change Impact

The purpose of **Assess the Change Impact** is to analyze how stakeholders will be impacted by the change and the change's specific impact on people, processes, tools, organizational structure, roles, and technology.

Standard for Change Management

This process involves identifying and categorizing who and what will be affected, assessing the degree of change occurring within these areas, and describing the change.

This process determines the size, scope, timing, and complexity of the change effort. It is used to inform and guide the formation of the change strategy and identify activities required to manage risk and resistance that may be associated with the change.

Inputs	Outputs
▸ Change Definition ▸ Vision Statement ▸ Research ▸ Stakeholder Analysis	▸ Change Impact Assessment

5.1.8 Assess Alignment of the Change with Organizational Strategic Objectives and Performance Measurement

The purpose of **Assess Alignment of the Change with Organizational Strategic Objectives and Performance Measurement** is to anticipate the impact of the expected benefits on the organization's strategic goals and objectives.

The process assesses where alignment and misalignment of objectives, targets, results, and performance measures occur between the future state and the current state. This is achieved by conducting a review of strategy with the relevant entities and individuals, such as those at the Executive Level, Strategic Planning Office, Change Management Office, and Project/Program Management Office. Strategic planning instruments such as balanced scorecards, strategic plans, and roadmaps should be evaluated and contrasted against the change being proposed.

Change management practitioners are responsible for driving appropriate actions to overcome obstacles and avoid or minimize adverse effects. The process identifies potential change obstacles and conflicts, as well as opportunities to manage or address them.

The process will produce one of four results:
▸ Confirm that change and strategy are in alignment
▸ Adapt strategy if change is deemed necessary but is insufficiently aligned with current strategy
▸ Postpone change until it is more aligned to organization strategy
▸ Cancel change

The result impacts the outputs produced or modified.

Inputs	Ouputs
▸ Strategic Plan ▸ Current Vision Statement ▸ Future State Vision Statement ▸ Case for Change ▸ Risk Plan	▸ Organizational Alignment Assessment ▸ Modifications to Organizational and Enterprise Performance Targets (Goals and Objectives) ▸ Modifications to Strategic Plan ▸ Modification of Business Case ▸ Modification of Vision Statement

Standard for Change Management©

5.1.9 Assess External Factors that May Affect Organizational Change

The purpose of **Assess External Factors that May Affect Organizational Change** is to identify the customer, market, social, legal, economic, political, technological, and other factors outside the organization that may influence stakeholder adoption of the future state.

This process is used to determine external factors that will enable or constrain the change effort and identify how those forces will influence the change approach. This is an iterative process because the external environment can introduce new risks or opportunities that can affect the change outcomes.

This process is used to guide and inform the development of the Change Management Strategy.

Inputs	Outputs
▸ Business Case ▸ Vision Statement ▸ Strategic Plan	▸ External Environment Impact Assessment

5.1.10 Assess Organization Culture(s) Related to the Change

The purpose of **Assess Organization Culture(s) Related to the Change** is to determine the cultural elements within the organization that may help or hinder the change direction and achievement of expected benefits. Organizational culture is defined as the shared values of and behaviors uniquely common to an organization. Organizational culture is integral in determining how tasks are completed, the way people interact with one another, the language they use when communicating, and the attitudes, goals, values, and leadership behaviors that are exhibited.

This process determines if the organization's current culture, structure, processes, and performance management system will support the change. If so, then the process will investigate how the current culture can be managed through the change. If the current culture will not support the change, then the process identifies the aspects of the current culture requiring change in order to realize the future state.

Indicators that a cultural change may be necessary to support and sustain the change include:
▸ Current culture does not allow stakeholders to work in ways that support the future state
▸ Current culture does not support the planned organizational process or behavior change
▸ Current values are in conflict with what will be expected of the stakeholders and leaders

The process focuses on the tangible cultural elements that regularly occur in an organization and the intangible elements, which are unwritten or unspoken beliefs and behaviors that may not be overt. The process identifies where cultural consistencies or compatibilities exist.

The Culture Assessment is used to guide and inform the development of the Change Management Strategy. The Culture Assessment findings can be used to anticipate and avoid roadblocks.

Copyright © 2019 Association of Change Management Professionals® (ACMP®) All Rights Reserved

Inputs	Outputs
▸ Core Values and Behaviors ▸ Current Communication Channels, Tools, and Methods ▸ Opinion Surveys and Feedback Assessments ▸ Vision Statement	▸ Culture Assessment

5.1.11 Assess Organizational Capacity for Change

The purpose of **Assess Organizational Capacity for Change** is to determine the ability of the various stakeholders impacted by the change to adopt the change and move toward the future state.

The capacity of an organization to adopt new changes is dependent on a variety of internal and external factors, including the organization's:

- Operational ability to absorb change
- Volume of concurrent changes (currently occurring and planned)
- Ability to absorb additional change
- Historical experience with change, including changes perceived as positive and negative
- Change maturity, which is the extent to which the organization uses change or project management methodologies, techniques, and tools
- Economic, environmental, and political stability (external and internal)

There are many methods and tools available to help the change management practitioner measure these factors, including:

- Perform a cultural assessment
- Review change and project management maturity audits
- Audit lessons learned and change, project, and portfolio reports to gauge an organization's current and planned changes and past record of adopting changes of similar magnitude
- Review independent reports on external and internal factors, including economy, environment, and political conditions

The required behavior changes, skill sets, competencies, and potential barriers to change may be identified, for example, by collaborating with leadership, line managers, human resources, and employees. These steps should be considered the pre-requisites for successful change because they will outline the minimum capacity the organization needs to achieve the proposed change.

Inputs	Outputs
▸ Competency Assessment ▸ Culture Assessment ▸ Organization's Historical Experience with Change ▸ Stakeholder Assessment ▸ External Environment Impact Assessment ▸ Change Impact Assessment ▸ Inventory of Change-Related Resources	▸ Organizational Change Capacity Assessment

5.1.12 Assess Organizational Readiness for Change

The purpose of **Assess Organizational Readiness for Change** is to determine the organization's preparedness for change activities.

This process assesses the preparedness of the conditions, attitudes, and resources needed for a change to happen successfully. This process should include organizational readiness elements, such as market factors, capacity, and saturation, which address key characteristics and attributes of the organization and the proposed change.

This process should also focus on assessing the organization's level of comprehension, perceptions, and expectations of the change. It should identify gaps existing between the change leaders' own skills, expectations, and attitudes, and the collective view of the organization. It should also assess the organizational process changes and determine the level of understanding and preparation of the organizational units for the transition.

This process is used to develop action plans if major weaknesses in the organization's readiness are identified.

Inputs	Outputs
▸ Change Objectives and Goals ▸ Culture Assessment ▸ Organizational Change Capacity Assessment ▸ Organizational Alignment Assessment ▸ Sponsorship Alignment Assessment ▸ Vision Statement ▸ Risk Assessment	▸ Organizational Change Readiness Assessment

5.1.13 Assess Communication Needs, Communication Channels, and Ability to Deliver Key Messages

The purpose of **Assess Communication Needs, Communication Channels, and Ability to Deliver Key Messages** is to determine the communication effort required to support the transition to the future state.

This process is used to define the communication needs of all stakeholders and focus on the specific communication needs of individuals or groups of stakeholders.

The Communication Needs Assessment is used to develop the Communication Strategy and to prepare resource and budget estimates. It is also used to identify risks that may directly affect communication effectiveness and progress toward change.

Inputs	Outputs
▸ Change Objectives and Goals ▸ Culture Assessment ▸ Organizational Change Capacity Assessment ▸ Sponsorship Alignment Assessment ▸ Stakeholder Analysis ▸ Current Communication Channels, Tools, and Methods ▸ Vision Statement ▸ Risk Assessment	▸ Communication Needs Assessment

5.1.14 Assess Learning Capabilities

The purpose of **Assess Learning Capabilities** is to determine the scale, magnitude, and complexity of the learning and development needed to ensure that the future state is successfully achieved.

The Learning Needs Assessment determines what stakeholders need to do differently and what will demonstrate the need for new competencies, capabilities, knowledge, skills, techniques, and behaviors required to successfully perform and sustain in the future state operations. It focuses on the future technical, social, and behavioral skills and abilities required. The process should determine the learning strategies and approaches and the need for learning equipment, educators, and logistics. It should also identify key constraints or barriers that may affect the learning program's success.

The Learning Needs Assessment is used to develop the Learning and Development Strategy. It is also used to prepare resource and budget estimates and performance metrics.

Inputs	Outputs
▸ Stakeholder Analysis ▸ Change Impact Assessment ▸ Communication Needs Assessment ▸ Culture Assessment ▸ Organizational Change Capacity ▸ Assessment ▸ Organizational Alignment Assessment	▸ Learning Needs Assessment

5.1.15 Conduct Change Risks Assessment

The purpose of **Conduct Change Risks Assessment** is to determine and anticipate the identifiable risks to the proposed change. These may be risks commonly associated with change, such as resistance of the stakeholders or lack of visible sponsorship from the leadership of the organization, but other possible risks that may affect the change should be considered. For example, the risk assessment might show a significant risk to successful implementation of the change unless certain stakeholders' roles change.

The assessment should include a level of measuring the impact of the identified risks on the change (e.g., whether a project would be completely halted should a risk become a reality).

Inputs	Outputs
▸ Stakeholder Analysis ▸ Change Impact Assessment ▸ Culture Assessment ▸ Organizational Change Capacity Assessment	▸ Change Risks Assessment ▸ Risk Register

5.2 Formulate the Change Management Strategy

The purpose of **Formulate the Change Management Strategy** is to develop the overarching approach for how an organization transitions from its current state to its future state. The

Change Management Strategy is typically designed to realize a set of goals to achieve specific organizational outcomes.

The Change Management Strategy details the scale, scope, and complexity of the change program and defines the requirements and implementation options, challenges, constraints, opportunities, success criteria, measurements, RACI, and governance for each change management activity needed to achieve successful and sustainable change implementation. It clarifies what needs to be done, why it needs to be done, who will do it, when it will be done, and the expected outcome. It may also include resource and other cost requirements for the change program, such as tools or technology solutions used by the change team, marketing/communication materials, or events.

The Change Management Strategy clearly states the Case for Change (sometimes referred to as the change case) and highlights program-specific approaches to develop and deliver all in-scope change management workstreams, which may include:

- Sponsor accountabilities and activities
- Leadership alignment
- Stakeholder engagement
- Communication
- Organization and process design
- Culture and behavior change
- Impact assessment and management
- Readiness planning
- Learning and development
- Performance management
- Risk management
- Benefit realization and sustainability management

The approach will be informed by the change diagnostics, assessments, and engagement completed in **5.1 Evaluate Change Impact and Organizational Readiness**. The diagnostics and assessments provide data for the change strategy to be tailored to the organization or to specific areas of the organization and are cognizant of the level of impact of change, challenges to implementing the change, communication barriers and opportunities, critical success factors, and engagement requirements.

Each organization will have unique constraints and opportunities that the change strategy must address. Key areas to be addressed in the change strategy to minimize risk to implementing the strategy and to maximize effectiveness include the following:

- **Strength of the Case for Change:** If the Case for Change is strong, well supported, and consistently communicated, then the level of risk will be lower because those affected will understand the need to make and commit to the required changes. If the strength of the case is weak, resulting in poor communication planning, low visibility, or minimal sponsorship support, then risk levels may be higher because those affected by the change will not "buy in" or accept the need to change. Inadequate change planning may result in poor adoption of the change, insufficient allocation of resources necessary to drive the change, and lack of credibility for the project.

- **Sponsorship engagement:** Clear and visible engagement and support from the sponsor has a direct impact on the success of the change. If the sponsor does not provide support, lacks active engagement in the change effort and activities, loses interest in the change efforts, or is distracted during the change efforts, then there should be intervention and risk management strategies in place to address the issue.
- **Degree that the success of the change depends on behavior changes:** Risk levels will be higher if change success depends on behavior changes than if the change does not require behavior changes, because behavior changes are harder to make compared to learning a new system or process. Inadequate assessment of the behavior change needed may result in lack of skill and capability to do things differently and misalignment with changegoals.
- **Degree that the success of the change depends on stakeholders learning a new skill:** The risk assessment should indicate the degree to which a change depends on the stakeholders learning a new skill. If stakeholders are capable of and have had experience with learning in the past, then the risk assessment should be lower.
- **Degree that the change affects stakeholders, customers, and vendors:** The level of change required by stakeholders, customers, and vendors can affect the level of risk. A high level of change represents a high degree of risk. Change success is at a greater risk when customers and vendors are affected by the change.
- **Amount of impact the change has on the organization's financial performance/health:** Greater financial dependence on change success increases the risk of change success and will likely shorten the time available to adopt the change. Therefore, results will likely need to be achieved quickly.
- **Amount of prior experience the organization has with change:** If the organization has past success with change and generally shows little resistance to change, then the risk should be lower. If the organization has past failures with change, then the risk will be higher.
- **Organizational alignment:** Misalignment of the organization's performance management practices, culture, organizational structure, and organizational design with the overall Change Management Strategy may result in a lack of readiness for the change, poor or slow adoption of the change, or stakeholders reverting to old ways.
- **Capacity for change:** The overall ability to make the change, such as workload or other change initiatives, based on environmental or timing factors.

The Change Management Strategy must be validated and approved by the change program sponsor and appropriate program team and organizational leadership. It may also require approval from organizational leaders, partners, and subject matter experts who have provided input to the strategy. In complex transformation programs, there may be a wide audience for the change strategy, including employee/colleague working councils or third-party suppliers. The strategy review and approval process should be clearly defined in the change program governance documents.

Questions to consider and respond to when developing the Change Management Strategy may include:
- Is the change incremental or transformational? Will the implementation be phased in or 'big bang'?
- Will the transition be linear and sequential, or will it require a multi-faceted, non-linear, non- sequential approach?

- How prepared is the organization for the change? What are the known and anticipated areas of resistance, and what mechanisms will be used to overcome them?
- What operational adjustments will be required to facilitate adoption of the change with minimal disruption?
- What mechanisms will be used to ensure the workforce has or acquires the skills and competencies required?
- Will technology components be required to facilitate the transition? If so, how will they be incorporated?
- How will workforce adjustment logistics be managed?
- What mechanisms will be used to ensure the necessary behaviors and attitudes have been adopted? How will progress be monitored?

5.2.1 Develop the Communication Strategy

The purpose of **Develop the Communication Strategy** is to create a strategy that, when executed, ensures that the organization and its customers are aware of and understand the organizational rationale for the change. It ensures that stakeholders are aligned regarding the program's expected value and benefits to the organization, initiation, progress, challenges, achievements, completion, and realized benefits. The Communication Strategy includes:

- The defined business rationale or Case for Change
- Stakeholders and sponsors
- Identified audiences, audience segmentation, and audience needs
- Targeted stakeholder messaging
- Identified communication channels and messaging frequency
- Identified feedback channels and loops
- Communication governance and review process

Communicate the Business Rationale

The Communication Strategy should include the business rationale for what, why, who, how, and when changes are taking place. It should provide the information detail necessary to enable change sponsors and the target audience to understand the key messages, channels, and frequency that the messages will be delivered during the change execution. Successful communication of the Case for Change occurs when business rationale communications are sufficient enough that each type and level of stakeholder can clearly articulate what is changing, how the change benefits or affects the organization, and how the change affects him or her individually (often referred to as "What's In It for Me"). If people see progress they can relate to, then they are more likely to continue the change effort and help to reach the future state and sustain the change.

Guiding Principles for Communication Messages

The Communication Strategy should provide guiding principles for communication messages. A message is a simple and clear idea and should summarize the essence of the change. Effective messaging means communicating the right message through the right channels. Messages should be relevant and appropriate to the audience, and there should be continuity across the messages. Using storytelling techniques that include interesting narratives, human interest stories, and arresting imagery will assist in communicating the message to the target audience.

Identify Communication Channels and Information Flow

The stakeholder group and sponsors should depict where and how information is shared within their respective organizations by mapping how communications will work throughout the organization.Channels for both formal and informal communication should be noted, and opportunities should be identified to include, leverage, and reinforce messaging content.

Considerations in developing an effective Communication Strategy include:
- Tailoring the communication activities to the needs
- Using message feedback
- Using push/pull/interactive communications
- Determining the best communication strategies (vertical/horizontal, verbal/non-verbal, informal/formal, oral/written, official/unofficial, internal/external)

Communication Governance and Review Process

The communication processes within organizations can have complex structures, with review and validation required by a number of groups (e.g., internal and external enterprise communication and legal, risk, and compliance teams), particularly where communications affect customers or third parties. The Communication Strategy should include the roles, responsibilities, accountabilities, resources, and timelines for communication content review and sign-off prior to publication.

Inputs	Outputs
▸ Change Definition ▸ Change Impact Assessment ▸ Current Communication Channels, Tools, and Methods ▸ Organizational Change Readiness Assessment ▸ Project Charter and Project Documentation ▸ Stakeholder Analysis ▸ Vision Statement	▸ Communication Strategy

5.2.2 Develop the Sponsorship Strategy

The purpose of **Develop the Sponsorship Strategy** is to create a high-level approach for preparing and leveraging the sponsors to promote, gain support for, and drive adoption of a change. Responsibility for developing the Sponsorship Strategy should be assigned to the Change Management Lead and include input from others who have knowledge of and experience with the sponsors.

Describe Why Sponsors Are Important

The Sponsorship Strategy should outline why sponsors are critical to the success of a change effort. Sponsors are critical to change success because:

Stakeholders want to learn about the change and the reasons for the change from the sponsors
- The importance stakeholders place on a change effort may be determined by the importance that sponsors demonstrate
- Sponsors build support for the change at all levels of the organization
- Sponsors can support identifying and mitigating risks associated with resistance to the change

Standard for Change Management©

- Sponsors provide the resources and budget, set expectations, and hold organizations and individuals accountable during the change
- Sponsors break down barriers and remove obstacles that restrict change implementation
- Sponsors provide consistent high-level messaging during the change program

Develop a High-Level Approach for Gaining Sponsorship Commitment

Sponsorship gaps that must be addressed for successful adoption of the change should be identified, and a high-level approach for addressing the gaps should be developed as early as possible. This high- level approach includes the activities to build a coalition of sponsorship that will drive and support the Sponsorship Strategy.

Risks to consider include a lack of sponsor commitment and support for the change, sponsorship competency gaps, and past sponsorship challenges.

Inputs	Outputs
- Change Risks - Organizational Change Readiness Assessment - Sponsorship Alignment Assessment - Stakeholder Analysis	- Sponsorship Strategy

5.2.3 Develop the Stakeholder Engagement Strategy

The purpose of **Develop the Stakeholder Engagement Strategy** is to identify an approach to ensure that individuals or groups impacted by a change and those who can positively affect the overall success of the change are engaged in the change effort. The core of stakeholder management and engagement includes taking the appropriate steps to identify stakeholders, conducting a Stakeholder Analysis, identifying the required engagement of the various stakeholders, and identifying the activities needed to achieve the required engagement.

Change stakeholders can be numerous and range from internal stakeholders like employees whose jobs are impacted by the changes to external stakeholders like customers or clients who might see or experience something differently because of the changes. A Stakeholder Engagement Strategy may not be appropriate for all change management efforts, but in more complex, large-scale change efforts, developing an overall direction and approach for stakeholder engagement helps to align and integrate stakeholder engagement plans, activities, requirements, and metrics.

Stakeholder engagement requires the attention and involvement of the people who will be impacted by the changes or who can influence the success of the changes and focuses on what the stakeholders and stakeholder groups need to know about the change and what they need to do. Good stakeholder engagement attracts and holds the attention of stakeholders to the degree needed for change success. The degree and type of stakeholder involvement required varies based on variables such as time, resource availability, negotiable elements within the future state, Change Management Strategy (directive versus collaborative), and stakeholder role. Depending on the change, a Stakeholder Engagement Strategy could include the identification of key stakeholders, prioritization of stakeholders, references to a Stakeholder Analysis, required stakeholder commitments, and methods for and appropriateness of soliciting stakeholder input.

Copyright © 2019 Association of Change Management Professionals® (ACMP®) All Rights Reserved

Inputs	Outputs
▸ Current State Analysis ▸ Change Impact Assessment ▸ Current Communication Channels, Tools, and Methods ▸ Communication Strategy ▸ Sponsorship Strategy ▸ Stakeholder Analysis	▸ Stakeholder Engagement Strategy

5.2.4 Develop the Change Impact and Readiness Strategy

The purpose of **Develop the Change Impact and Readiness Strategy** is to define the approach, scope, roles, and responsibilities in undertaking detailed impact analysis and readiness planning for implementing the change. Understanding the specific impacts on people, processes, tools, organizational structure, job roles, and technology will inform all areas of the change strategy and is critical for developing the Training Strategy and Readiness Strategy.

The Readiness Strategy focuses on what actions and activities need to be completed in advance of the change being implemented. It includes the readiness criteria for implementation, the governance structure, and accountability for readiness activities that will determine if the organization is ready to accept the change. Readiness management is a critical activity that supports projects meeting key pre- implementation milestones and ensures a smooth transition to new ways of working.

Inputs	Outputs
▸ Stakeholder Engagement Strategy ▸ Change Impact Assessment	▸ Change Impact and Readiness Strategy

5.2.5 Develop the Learning and Development Strategy

The purpose of **Develop the Learning and Development Strategy** is to define the knowledge, skills, and competencies required for stakeholders to adopt the change, which informs creation and delivery of learning and development programs and training courses. The key components that the Learning and Development Strategy identifies are the skills and competencies needed to perform in the changed environment, those needing training to close the competency gap, the content to be delivered, the method of delivery, and methods to determine the effectiveness of the training.

Demonstrating the Need

The Learning and Development Strategy should document what stakeholders must be able to do differently because of the change and how they need to be able to work to be successful in the future state. The strategy ensures that impacted stakeholders are equipped with the necessary knowledge, skills, and abilities to achieve the future state.

Defining a High-Level Approach

The Learning and Development Strategy should define a high-level approach that ensures understanding of the intended work effort.

Explaining different learning and development methods and tools: The learning and development method is dependent upon the type of change and culture of the organization. It should identify the most effective learning and development methods and tools when defining the high-level approach. Key learning and development methods may include:
- Instructor-led (face-to-face and virtual)
- Computer-based
- Webcasts/Podcasts
- Role plays
- Simulations
- On-the-job
- Gamification

Identifying possible resources: Some organizations have internal learning and development departments that can be leveraged to conduct the learning and development. Other organizations will rely on external consulting expertise or outsourcing to conduct these activities. The high-level approach should outline the resourcing plan to conduct the learning and development activities.

Estimating a timeline: The high-level plan should include an estimated timeline for the learning and development that aligns with the project schedule. Learning and development should be close enough to the actual change that stakeholders will remember what they learned and be able to transfer the new skills to their jobs.

Identifying proposed deliverables: The expected learning and development deliverables and supporting materials need to be defined in the Learning and Development Strategy. This will establish the work effort expected to complete learning and development. Deliverables may include a learning and development plan, curriculum, materials (e.g., user manual, quick reference guide), and an evaluation.

Key considerations in defining the learning and development approach may include:
- License costs for training tools
- Commissioning training environments to deliver training of new technical or digital solutions
- Data used in training material and any data privacy requirements
- An approach to piloting the training in advance of deployment to ensure it is fit for purpose
- Governance for sign-off of training content, particularly if there is a legal or regulatory requirement
- An approach to transitioning training from the change program to "business as usual" training, including knowledge transfer and management

Determine Evaluation Techniques

There are a wide variety of approaches and techniques to evaluate learning activities. The Learning and Development Strategy should explain the importance of evaluating learning and development and how it should be approached. Measuring the success of a learning and development program demonstrates whether the participants learned the skills needed. The learning objectives should be used to define training content and measure adoption after training. Identifying the objectives of the learning and development program prior to the delivery also enables the change practitioner to evaluate adoption success after training completion.

Inputs	Outputs
▸ Learning Needs Assessment ▸ Stakeholder Analysis	▸ Learning and Development Strategy

5.2.6 Develop the Measurement and Benefit Realization Strategy

The purpose of **Develop the Measurement and Benefit Realization Strategy** is to define success criteria and measures to monitor whether the change is achieving its expected benefits and to adapt the change effect as needed.

It is important to begin measuring as early as possible in the lifecycle of the effort. This provides timely information to gauge the effectiveness of the change strategy, keep the change implementation on track, allow for course correction, and ensure that organizational benefits defined in the project charter are realized.

Develop the Measurement Strategy: The change objectives and goals should be used to determine what is required to achieve the future state. These targets should be specific and quantifiable for the organization to understand what is expected.

Another aspect of the Measurement Strategy is to assess the effectiveness of the strategy used to drive the change effort itself. Common areas of focus include communication and learning to allow for refinement as needed. Techniques can include stakeholder surveys and feedback from line managers, change agents, and focus groups.

Benefit Realization Strategy: Mechanisms must be installed to monitor the achievement of the performance targets. These mechanisms include developing the process, data collection, and reporting requirements for each measure.

The components of the Benefit Realization Strategy are:
- Assigning owners for each measure and target
- Determining when and how the measurement data will be collected, the reporting frequency, and how information will be shared
- Creating an approach to address slippage or slow attainment of measure
- Aligning with reward strategies
- Establishing timelines for addressing issues related to achieving the targets
- Communicating performance targets to the organization

Inputs	Outputs
▸ Strategic Plan ▸ Case for Change ▸ Change Objectives and Goals ▸ Project Charter ▸ Success Criteria	▸ Measurement and Benefit Realization Strategy ▸ Revised Performance and Rewards Targets

5.2.7 Develop the Sustainability Strategy

The purpose of **Develop the Sustainability Strategy** is to describe how the change will become part of the organization's normal functioning. It should define the high-level approach for embedding or institutionalizing the change to achieve the expected benefits and include all streams of change management activity, such as communication and engagement, metrics tracking, performance management, reward and recognition, learning and development, sustaining ownership, and continuous improvement.

The Sustainability Strategy details the approach to embedding the change in the organization once the program has delivered the change. It defines the sustainability evaluation criteria, including performance metrics, cultural indicators, desired employee/customer behaviors, key performance indicators, scorecards, transactional volumes, exception rates, customer satisfaction scores, and employee temperature checks. It may also include sustainment activities for change support functions.

The Sustainability Strategy defines the scope, scale, roles, responsibilities, resource requirements, accountability, and governance structure for the sustainment program. It provides a clear roadmap for maintaining the formal or informal networks or communities of practice that have supported the change initiative and outlines a long-term plan for ongoing knowledge management. Key inputs to the Sustainability Strategy are the lessons learned from each phase of the change program.

The Sustainability Strategy should cover:

- Communication (ongoing socialization of the change)
- Metrics tracking
- Performance management
- Rewards and recognition (linking rewards and recognition to behaviors required by the change)
- Sustained ownership (ensuring experience and knowledge transfer
- Knowledge transfer (consistent and effective process for assessing stakeholder and organizational competencies and the systems, structures, and mechanisms needed to ensure stakeholders develop the skills and motivation to perform as expected in the changed environment)
- Continuous process improvement

Inputs	Outputs
- Business Case - Change Objectives and Goals - Change Risk Assessment - Project Charter and Documentation - Strategic Plan - Success Criteria and Measures	- Sustainability Strategy

Standard for Change Management©

5.3 Develop the Change Management Plan

The purpose of **Develop the Change Management Plan** is to document the actions, timelines, and resources needed to deliver the change. The Change Management Strategy provides the "why" and the "what," and the Change Management Plan provides the "how." The Change Management Plan is a series of component plans that define the scope of the change effort and how it will be undertaken, controlled, and monitored.

The Change Management Plan should reflect the overall complexity of the change effort and consider:

- Objectives/goals and intended outcomes of the change effort defined in **5.1 Evaluate Change Impact and Organizational Readiness**
- Steps to address the change and by whom
- How to facilitate the change effort
- How the change management effort will be implemented, transitioned, and sustained
- Dependencies of the change plan activities
- Assumptions, issues, and risks

When developing the Change Management Plan, questions to consider and respond to may include:

- What mechanisms will be used to ensure the workforce has or acquires the required skills and competencies?
- Will technology components be required to facilitate the transition? If so, how will they be incorporated?
- How will workforce adjustment logistics be managed?
- What mechanisms will be used to ensure the necessary behaviors and attitudes have been adopted? How will progress be monitored?

5.3.1 Develop a Comprehensive Change Management Plan

The **Change Management Plan** should include required actions and baseline measures as they pertain to a change effort's scope, expected benefits, role requirements, resources, activity schedule, risk, and measurement. The level of detail of the Change Management Plan should reflect the complexity and risk of the change effort.

Key components of the Change Management Plan include:

- **Resource Plan:** Defines what resources (e.g., people, capability or skill sets, location, equipment) will be necessary to accomplish the tasks.
- **Sponsorship Plan:** Identifies the change sponsors and defines a course of action to develop and strengthen the competencies required to effectively lead/sponsor a change initiative.
- **Stakeholder Engagement Plan:** Identifies actions to engage groups and individuals affected by the change and then mitigate their resistance to and enlist their support, adoption, and ownership of the change.
- **Communication Plan:** Defines internal and external audiences, information, and feedback requirements of those leading and affected by the change, and specific communication activities and events.

Copyright © 2019 Association of Change Management Professionals® (ACMP®) All Rights Reserved

- **Impact Assessment and Readiness Plan:** Identifies the actions, roles, and responsibilities for detailed impact analysis following the high-level impact analysis undertaken in the assessment phase described in **5.1 Evaluate Change Impact and Organizational Readiness**. It details how and when impacts will be captured during the design, build, and implement phase of the project, including impact categorization and mapping and ownership of impact mitigation and management. The Readiness Plan identifies the organization/customer readiness criteria and readiness management approach.

- **Learning and Development Plan:** Identifies needs and knowledge gaps of those affected by the change and provides a course of action to prepare end users with the skills and knowledge necessary to navigate the change.

- **Measurement and Benefit Realization Plan:** Defines processes and actions to monitor and track progress on the project's key performance indicators as defined in the project charter and identifies when mitigation strategies need to be implemented if the change effort falls short of its goals.

- **Sustainability Plan:** Provides an approach to maintaining the new processes and achieving a day-to-day method of doing business once the change has become a way of working and business as usual.

The Change Management Plan will be shared and reviewed with key stakeholders and should be continually monitored and updated as needed.

The following sections provide the specific details of the component plans.

5.3.1.1 Resource Plan

The **Resource Plan** defines the human, physical, and financial resources needed to implement the expected benefits of the change effort. It identifies how to acquire resources and a timeline for resource utilization. The following sections describe the key components of the Resource Plan.

Human Resources

The Resource Plan defines the type of labor needed to support the change management effort. Defining roles and responsibilities for each type of labor ensures that individuals with certain skills and capabilities are in the right roles and performing the requisite tasks. These individuals range from the executive support/sponsor driving the change effort and individuals responsible for leading the change effort to those providing support and participating on the change management team.

To ensure that the correct resources fill key roles in the change effort, skills and capabilities must be defined, along with the number of people required for each role. One person may have multiple roles depending on the scope of change, size of the organization, geography, and other factors. The next step is to perform a gap analysis to determine if the skills required exist in the organization and can be filled by a stakeholder, or if third-party service providers (e.g., consultants) will be required. The final step is to create a staffing plan that assigns roles and individuals to specific change management tasks.

Physical Resources

The Resource Plan determines the physical resources needed to support the change effort. Internal resources or external vendors can provide physical resources such as systems hardware, software, and other technical infrastructure, as well as facilities, workspace, furniture, or other physical needs for accomplishing the initiative goals.

Financial Resources

The Resource Plan ensures the costs of all resources supporting the change effort are appropriately budgeted for and approved in the overall project plan.

The costs associated with the Resource Plan will adhere to a defined review and approval process. The resources identified in the plan will be budgeted and staffed as part of the overall project plan.

Inputs	Outputs
▸ Change Management Resources, Roles, and Responsibilities Strategy ▸ Communication Strategy ▸ Learning and Development Strategy ▸ Change Resources Inventory ▸ Procurement Guidelines and Policies	▸ Resource Plan

5.3.1.2 Sponsorship Plan

The **Sponsorship Plan** should define how to identify, develop, and strengthen the competencies required to lead/sponsor a change initiative. This plan builds awareness, establishes understanding, and defines leader/sponsor core responsibilities in a change management activity. If a sponsor is resistant to any of the responsibilities, then these issues must be addressed in the early stages.

Key components of a Sponsorship Plan include:
▸ Definition of specific responsibilities for leaders/sponsors
▸ Agreement by leaders/sponsors regarding their responsibilities, including how they will work with others engaged in the change activity
▸ Learning and development plan for the leaders/sponsors

Inputs	Outputs
▸ Sponsorship Strategy ▸ Sponsorship Alignment Assessment ▸ Stakeholder Analysis ▸ Sponsor Assessment	▸ Sponsorship Plan

5.3.1.3 Stakeholder Engagement Plan

The **Stakeholder Engagement Plan** outlines the activities and metrics that will be established to ensure stakeholders and stakeholder groups can make the changes required or complete the steps that will help make change successful in an organization.

Stakeholder engagement activities are designed to address the outcomes of a Stakeholder Analysis. The Stakeholder Analysis identifies gaps between the current state of a stakeholder or stakeholder group and the future state. In order for successful organizational change to occur, the gaps that exist between current and future states need to be eliminated. A good Stakeholder Analysis identifies the key components of those gaps, and the stakeholder engagement plan provides the relevant activities to address components and close the gaps.

A number of tactics can be employed in a Stakeholder Engagement Plan. The most common activities include formal, two-way, and informal communication; learning, development, training, and discovery activities; and rewards, recognition, reinforcement, and consequences. Successful stakeholder engagement plans include clear metrics to ensure that the plan is meeting the intended outcomes. A number of factors should be considered when designing stakeholder engagement activities, including organizational culture, other change initiatives affecting stakeholders, activities that will get and keep a stakeholder's attention, stakeholder needs, and the specific engagement required for successful change to occur in a stakeholder or group.

As with many of the components of a well-managed change, Stakeholder Analysis and Stakeholder Engagement Plans are iterative. Stakeholder Engagement Plans are updated as needed and adjusted based on metrics measuring the effectiveness of the activities.

Stakeholder Engagement Plans also include activities designed to drive the behavior of stakeholders that can affect the overall success of the change. These types of activities can include tools, templates, and key messages that enable stakeholders to customize and personalize their behavior and messaging to the employees that they are trying to impact. These activities and their timing are driven by factors such as the project plan, project timing, position or potential impact of the stakeholder or stakeholder group, and the status of the overall change at any given moment. Stakeholder engagement plan activities should align with sponsorship plans. A clearer and most holistic message can be received when change sponsors and influential stakeholders deliver consistent messages.

Inputs	Outputs
▸ Stakeholder Analysis ▸ Stakeholder Engagement Strategy ▸ Communication Strategy ▸ Sponsorship Strategy ▸ Change Risks	▸ Stakeholder Engagement Plan

5.3.1.4 Communication Plan

The **Communication Plan** defines the internal and external audiences, information, and feedback requirements of those leading and affected by the change, as well as the specific communication activities and events.

Strategic communication activities may include messaging that addresses the Case for Change, how the change aligns with the organizational strategy, why the change is occurring, intended outcomes, benefits of the change, and the risks or consequences of a failed effort. More tactical communications could include status reports and "how to" guides for technology changes. The Communication Plan should include all actions needed to build awareness of the change and clearly outline what is expected from people affected by the change.

The Communication Plan includes key components such as:

- **Target Audience(s):** Segments the stakeholder audiences according to demographics, outcomes, and the roles stakeholder groups may have in a change effort. There are often multiple stakeholder groups with different communication needs, and communications should be developed accordingly. The audiences should encompass stakeholders directly impacted by the change, along with those not impacted but who should be aware of the change.

- **Outcomes:** Defines what the audience should know, think, and do because of communication actions. Some communications may be for informational purposes only, whereas others may be required to drive desirable behaviors.

- **Sender:** Identifies from whom the communication will come. Strategic communications should come from organizational leadership or other key leaders to ensure maximum impact. The Change Sponsor typically communicates regarding topics that define the change, and the sponsor should demonstrate support. Other leaders or the change team may communicate directly to stakeholder groups for tactical communications.

- **Key Messages:** Describes the words and visuals that will drive achievement of the intended communication goal for each unique stakeholder group.

- **Communications Channels:** Identifies the specific ways that information is distributed to and received back from stakeholder audiences. Channels should be selected based on their potential effectiveness in reaching each target audience. For maximum effectiveness, channel selection should factor in the purpose of communication, audience demographics, content, messaging, and interaction or feedback requirements. Examples of communication channels include email, social media, town halls, webinars, meetings, intranets, collaboration sites, video, newsletters, posters, and digital signage. Most change activities require that multiple channels be used for effective communication. An effective Communication Plan should allow for two-way conversations that provide opportunities for conversation and dialogue.

- **Frequency:** Specifies the number of times key messages will be communicated in selected channels. Most change activities require a relatively high frequency of messages being communicated to stakeholder audiences

- **Timing**: Defines the schedule for communication activities. This ensures the timeliness of communications and prevents communication overlap from multiple stakeholders. Reviewing non-project communications against the change communication plan can avoid saturation.

- **Costs and Resources**: Identifies the resources and associated costs needed to produce and distribute the communications. These costs should be integrated into the overall project budget.

- **Reviewers and Approvers**: Identifies the individuals who need to review and approve the plan.

- **Monitoring and Feedback**: Monitoring and adjusting the Communication Plan ensures continued effectiveness to achieve the expected benefits of the change effort. Clearly defined feedback mechanisms (e.g., surveys, focus groups, help desk tickets) assess the effectiveness of the plan. Communications may need modification to address cultural norms of a diverse workforce.

Standard for Change Management©

Inputs	Outputs
▸ Communication Strategy ▸ Current Communication Channels, Tools, and Methods ▸ Key Messages ▸ Learning and Development Strategy ▸ Project Charter and Documentation ▸ Project Schedule and Plan ▸ Sponsorship Strategy ▸ Stakeholder Analysis ▸ Stakeholder Engagement Strategy ▸ Transition Strategy	▸ Communication Plan

5.3.1.5 Learning and Development Plan

The **Learning and Development Plan** identifies knowledge gaps and training needs of those affected by the change and then provides a course of action to develop end users so they will be prepared with new knowledge and skills to adopt the change successfully.

Key components of the Learning and Development Plan include:
- Learning groups
- Learning curriculum
- Skills inventory and gap analysis for each learning group
- Ongoing learning tools (e.g., job aids, quick tips, Frequently Asked Questions, refresher guides)
- Learning delivery plan
- Learning evaluation and optimization plan

Learning and development design and delivery should be continually assessed and adjusted as needed to ensure continued effectiveness to achieve the expected benefits of the change effort. The plan should identify additional training and other learning resources as new phases or processes are introduced.

Inputs	Outputs
▸ Learning and Development Strategy ▸ Stakeholder Analysis ▸ Learning Needs Assessment	▸ Learning and Development Plan

5.3.1.6 Measurement and Benefit Realization Plan

The **Measurement and Benefit Realization Plan** defines processes and actions to monitor and track progress of the project's key performance indicators and expected benefits, as stated in the Project Charter and Strategy Plan. The Measurement and Benefit Realization Plan provides a means of identifying when mitigation strategies need to be implemented if the effort is falling short of its goals.

The Measurement and Benefit Realization Plan should include current baseline performance on key objectives and goals and track how those key indicators/objectives are affected throughout the change effort. It should specify measurement activities that provide valid and reliable data for tracking activity and effects on performance.

Copyright © 2019 Association of Change Management Professionals® (ACMP®) All Rights Reserved

Key components of a Measurement and Benefit Realization Plan include:
- A schedule of measurement activities, including type, frequency, how conducted, and by whom
- A report template for reporting measurement results at defined intervals to defined groups and individuals who own the metrics and are responsible for taking action to ensure targets are achieved

Inputs	Outputs
- Measurement and Benefit Realization Strategy - Change Definition - Change Objectives and Goals - Vision Statement	- Measurement and Benefit Realization Plan

5.3.1.7 Sustainability Plan

A **Sustainability Plan** should be developed to define the mechanisms that will be used to anchor and embed the change once it is implemented and is determined to be effective.

The Sustainability Plan should minimally include the following components:
- **Communication:** Mechanisms for persuasive communication and ongoing socialization of the change, rites of parting (saying goodbye to the old ways of doing things), and rites of enhancement (acknowledgment of quick wins and continued adoption)
- **Metrics Tracking:** Consistent and effective process for ongoing measurement and results reporting to track progress and ensure sustained results
- **Performance Management:** Consistent process for observing and objectively measuring desired behaviors and attitudes, including performance appraisal process, promoting, demoting and transferring, and training and development
- **Rewards and Recognition:** Program of intrinsic and extrinsic incentives to reinforce desired behaviors and attitudes
- **Sustaining Ownership:** Consistent process for ensuring sustained ownership of the change through the ongoing transfer of experience and knowledge
- **Continuous Improvement:** Mechanisms for responding to changing requirements and implementing improvements based on feedback, observations, and metrics

Questions to consider and respond to when developing the Sustainability Plan may include:
- How should organizational achievements reinforcing the change be commemorated?
- What behaviors should be observed and measured on a regular basis?
- What results should be observed and measured on a regular basis?
- What metrics should be used for measuring behaviors and results?
- What mechanisms should be used for reporting results?
- What criteria should be used to allocate rewards and promotion?
- What mechanisms should be used for training, coaching, and role modeling?
- What processes and procedures should be put in place to ensure sustained ownership of the change?
- What continuous improvement mechanisms will address low adoption rates and ensure the change becomes part of the organization's normal functioning?

Inputs	Outputs
▸ Status Report/Benefits Gap Analysis ▸ Resource Plan	▸ Sustainability Plan

5.3.2 Integrate Change Management and Project Management Plans

The relationship between Change Management and Project Management is highly dependent on the nature of the change program, as defined in **4.4 Relationship to Project Management**.

It is recommended that the relationship between Project Management and Change Management be defined early in the project, when the governance structure is established. Common structures include Project Management and Change Management professionals functioning as peers and aligning their activities or positioning Change Management as a part of the Project Team with its own workstream.

Integrating the Project Management and Change Management Plans can ensure stakeholders in the organization align efforts to facilitate adoption of the change. Integration may occur along the following dimensions:

- **Roles and Responsibilities:** Define the relationship of the change management team to the overall project team and clarify the responsibilities of each. A collaborative partnership should be established to maximize a successful outcome of the overall effort.
- **Methodology and Plan:** Follow a structured methodology that aligns with the overall project management methodology. Change Management efforts should begin in the project initiation phase.
- **Tools and Resources:** Seek opportunities to leverage common tools across both disciplines for a holistic approach. The communication plan, risk assessment/mitigation plans, and resource plans are common tools to leverage across Change Management and Project Management.
- **Objectives and Outcomes:** Establish and integrate change management objectives regarding adoption and usage into overall project plan objectives.
- **Risks**: Address risks that are specifically related to stakeholders (e.g., resistance risks). Responsibility for tracking and mitigating risks, especially stakeholder-related risks, should be determined early in the project.

The Change Management Lead will monitor the Change Management Plan to ensure alignment with the project and communicate updates to the appropriate team members.

Inputs	Outputs
▸ Change Management Plan ▸ Project Charter and Project Documentation ▸ Project Schedule and Plan	▸ Change Management Plan (updated) ▸ Project Plan (updated)

5.3.3 Review and Approve the Change Management Plan in Collaboration with Project Leadership

The objective of **Review and Approve the Change Plan in Collaboration with Project Leadership** is to ensure that project leadership is aware of and aligned with milestones in the Change Management Plan.

Review and approval of the Change Management Plan is necessary to ensure that it is incorporated into the Project Plan and that the activities and milestones are coordinated with project activities.

Collaboration with project leadership is essential to avoid duplication of effort, align work plans, and increase stakeholder awareness.

Inputs	Outputs
▸ Change Management Plan ▸ Project Plan	▸ Change Management Plan (approved)

5.3.4 Develop Feedback Mechanisms to Monitor Performance to Plan

Monitoring performance and adherence to deliverables generated from the Change Management Plan enables adjustments of the plan in response to performance. Changes to the overall Project Plan, as well as unexpected outcomes and changes in scope, will influence the Change Management Plan.

Feedback will come from many sources. Informal sources of feedback may include conversations, email responses, and information-sharing forums. Feedback mechanisms collect formal feedback and enable the team to develop responses and monitor the effectiveness of the Change Management Plan.

Feedback should be collected frequently and be scheduled for appropriate intervals for the purpose of data comparisons. Collected information should be shared with the project leadership team and incorporated into the planning of future change management activities.

Inputs	Outputs
▸ Communication Plan ▸ Learning and Development Plan ▸ Measurement and Benefit Realization Plan ▸ Project Schedule and Plan ▸ Stakeholder Engagement Plan	▸ Communication Plan (updated) ▸ Learning and Development Plan (updated) ▸ Measurement and Benefit Realization Plan (updated) ▸ Stakeholder Engagement Plan (updated)

5.4 Execute the Change Management Plan

The purpose of **Execute the Change Management Plan** is to address the implementation processes for performing the change activities by monitoring, measuring, and controlling delivery against baseline plans.

Standard for Change Management[©]

The Change Management Plan defines how internal controls will be applied. It involves managing people (stakeholders and sponsors) and other resources while developing employee competencies through learning, development, and knowledge transfer.

Executing the Change Management Plan involves alignment of strategic objectives, risk identification, and mitigation and modification of the plan as needed.

5.4.1 Execute, Manage, and Monitor Implementation of the Change Management Plan

Execute, Manage, and Monitor Implementation of the Change Management Plan requires that all resources, strategies, timelines, communications, and learnings combine to carry out the intended purpose of the Change Management Plan. It applies the processes identified through assessments and analyses to the needs of completing tasks and activities of the Change Management Plan.

5.4.1.1 Execute Resource Plan

Executing the coordination of finances, people, information, and physical resources is necessary to ensure delivery of the Resource Plan.

Financial Resources Management

During execution, the planned budget for the change will be controlled so that accountable spending to meet the deliverables can take place. It may be necessary to review the planned budget in the light of additional information as execution begins. This may require an increase, decrease, or reallocation of the budget between spending categories, executed through a controlled request process and approved by appropriate stakeholders.

The spending process should be documented and understood by all involved, especially those providing control over the spending. Controls will include type and amount of spending.

Regular reports of spending against budget should be prepared for senior stakeholders to ensure transparency.

Human Resources Management

Human resources management is a strategic function for identifying the most effective use of people. Expected benefits can be delayed, diminished, or never realized if the proper human resources are not available when they need to deliver and embed the change.

Resource availability conflicts may occur due to competing priorities, coinciding tasks, or unavoidable circumstances. These conflicts may require rescheduling activities and could result in changes in resource requirements for current or subsequent activities. Procedures should be established to identify such shortages, facilitate resource reallocation, and reduce the likelihood and consequence of resource availability conflicts.

Specific role definitions should be defined, along with their required skill sets, experience levels, and engagement durations. The engagement processes for different types of resources (e.g., permanent employees, contractors, consultants) need to be fully defined, understood, and documented to enable execution of the human resources plan.

Copyright © 2019 Association of Change Management Professionals® (ACMP®) All Rights Reserved

Human resources should be recruited, selected, and oriented to the project and integrated with the change team in order to build change capability and support the resources plan.

Information Resources Management

Information resources management involves a systematic process for creating, storing, sharing, and disseminating data records, documents, and reports related to the Change Management effort.

Processes should be established for authorizing which stakeholder groups can create, review, update, or delete certain types of records, documents, and reports. It is expected and acceptable that confidential and other types of records, documents, and reports would not be accessible to stakeholders impacted by a change. Information repositories (e.g., electronic file sharing system, collaborative website, physical documents) can provide appropriate security access for specific stakeholder groups.

Organization resources that may provide assistance include the Information Technology/Services (IT/IS) function and the Legal/Records Retention function.

Physical Resources Management

Physical resources management involves ensuring the availability of suitable facilities, equipment, and supplies. The primary functions include identifying what is required and ensuring that suppliers provide equipment and materials needed to deliver the change. It also involves managing the purchasing relationship, which includes negotiating with suppliers to reach agreements that provide value and meet organizational requirements, keeping accurate records of materials, and taking appropriate action in the event of problems with the materials.

Processes should be established to monitor physical resources and their performance. These processes will ensure the standards of service and delivery are maintained, physical resources are used efficiently, and suppliers are delivering the desired activities and outcomes.

Resources such as buildings, rooms, technology, and other physical needs should be acquired to support the execution of the plan. Physical resources must meet the needs specified during planning and cover areas such as quality, quantity, and duration. They should be engaged or acquired through an agreed- upon, documented control process to ensure that needs are met and value is obtained.

Inputs	Outputs
▸ Change Management Plan ▸ Project Schedule and Plan ▸ Resource Plan	▸ Change Management Plan ▸ Financial Resources Update/Impact Reports ▸ Human Resources Update/Impact Reports ▸ Information Resources Update/Impact Reports ▸ Physical Resources Update/Impact ▸ Reports

5.4.1.2 Execute Communication Plan

The success of a Change Management Program requires effective implementation of the **Communication Plan.**

Execute the Established Communication Plan

The audience and its specific characteristics (e.g., size of the organization, location of workers, level of change resistance) serve as the basis for customizing the messaging and delivery methods. The message should be crafted considering the culture of the stakeholders and organization and be aligned with the objective for each communication event. When effective, the stakeholders are able to build awareness, establish understanding, and define core responsibilities around the delivery of messages.

Delivery of Messaging

Messages are delivered through the method deemed most effective for the communication. Further, messages are delivered at a specific phase in the project to ensure that stakeholders receive the correct messages at the correct time. Communication subject matter experts may provide guidance in the delivery of the communications and regularly assess effectiveness.

Feedback

The feedback channels and mechanisms identified in the Communication Strategy should be executed, as they provide stakeholders with the opportunity to ask questions and provide updates on how they are experiencing the change.

Inputs	Outputs
▸ Project Plan ▸ Communication Plan ▸ Stakeholder Engagement Plan	▸ Communication Delivery

5.4.1.3 Execute Sponsorship Plan

Sponsorship is most successful when leaders recognize the people side of change and visibly participate with stakeholders throughout the project. The change sponsor builds awareness directly with stakeholders regarding the need for the change.

Prepare Sponsors

The change management team reviews the role of sponsorship with each leader involved in the change initiative and provides change management coaching where needed. Coaching should address the need for sponsors to understand their role, responsibilities, and expectations and include identifiable actions that visibly support successful change, examples of good sponsorship activities, and common sponsor mistakes. The sponsor should also receive prepared communications and guidance for delivering messages to stakeholder groups.

Sustain Sponsor Engagement

The Change Management Lead should provide the sponsor with regular updates on the change initiative status.

Inputs	Outputs
▸ Sponsorship Plan ▸ Communication Plan ▸ Stakeholder Engagement Plan	▸ Sponsor Activities ▸ Sponsor Competency Building Activities

5.4.1.4 Execute Stakeholder Engagement Plan

Effective stakeholder engagement is critical to ensure successful execution of the Change Management Plan.

The Stakeholder Engagement Plan establishes the tasks that need to be executed to ensure that all stakeholders understand and adopt the change. Executing the plan will significantly reduce uncertain consequences and identify the benefits of the change for stakeholders. Effective plan execution will enable stakeholders to adopt the change swiftly and with lowered resistance, while understanding its benefits to the organization and individual stakeholder.

Resistance Management

Addressing and managing resistance to ensure successful transition to the future state should engage a number of leaders within the organization. Key aspects of job roles, performance management, learning needs, and organizational development resources should be considered and reviewed regularly throughout the change initiative. These reviews should involve regular communication with leaders and supporting functions as needed to ensure resistance is properly managed.

Inputs	Outputs
▸ Stakeholder Engagement Plan ▸ Sponsorship Plan ▸ Communication Plan	▸ Stakeholder Engagement Activities ▸ Sponsor Engagement Activities ▸ Resistance Management Activities

5.4.1.5 Execute Learning and Development Plan

Change initiatives require active management of the learning process to increase stakeholder skills and develop required competencies through appropriate learning activities. Learning and development may include training and development activities as well as evaluating knowledge, skills, and attitudes before and after the learning activities.

Define Learning Objectives

Learning objectives should be clearly stated, measurable, realistic, and appropriate for the level of the learner. They should be consistent with the objectives of the Change Management Strategy and define what the learner will know or be able to do because of the learning activity. They should provide a basis to evaluate learner achievement.

Execute Learning and Development Plan

As stated in **5.3.1.5 Learning and Development Plan**, each learning group has a unique curriculum that will be executed. The first step in executing the plan is to ensure the learning materials supporting the curriculum have been developed (e.g., job aids, user manuals, quick reference guides). Second, the logistics of the learning activity for each group must be completed according to the delivery method and timeline (e.g., booking a conference room, setting up an online meeting). Lastly, the curriculum is delivered to the specified group according to the plan. As stated in the Learning and Development Strategy, there may be other resources such as an outside vendor delivering the learning activity.

Evaluate Learning Activities

Measuring the success of learning and development activities demonstrates whether the participants learned the necessary skills. The objectives developed prior to delivery will serve as the basis for the evaluation.

Not all learning activities will deliver the expected benefits, possibly because a lesson was misunderstood, misapplied, or was not applicable to the situation or audience. Learning activities that do not produce the expected benefits should be reevaluated and then modified or removed.

Learning measurement should determine what knowledge was obtained, the skills that were developed or improved, and the frequency and effectiveness with which the new knowledge and skills are used on the job. It may also identify if attitudes have changed. A variety of methods can be used to evaluate the effects of learning, including learner reactions, supervisor observations, and performance appraisals.

The evaluation should show both the tangible and intangible indicators resulting from the learning and development activities.

Tangible Indicators	Intangible Indicators
▸ Skills and knowledge ▸ Job performance ▸ Productivity ▸ Response time ▸ Sales volume and service levels ▸ Requests for help	▸ Effective communication ▸ Quality of decision making ▸ Conducive teamwork ▸ Job satisfaction ▸ Stress rate

Inputs	Outputs
▸ Learning and Development Plan ▸ Change Resources, Roles, and Responsibilities Plan ▸ Supporting Learning and Development ▸ Materials (e.g., job aids)	▸ Learning and Performance Evaluation Reports

5.4.1.6 Execute Measurement and Benefit Realization

Accurate measurements provide an indication of the level of stakeholder adoption, the degree of stakeholder preparedness (knowledge and ability), and the success of the change project. The measurements should be communicated to all sponsors and project leads. Processes can be adapted based on the measurement outcomes to ensure that goals are met.

Tracking and Measuring Benefits

This process involves tracking and measuring the benefits against targets to ensure changes are aligned with organizational objectives and expected benefits as described in the business case. It involves measuring against the baseline data and target, charting progress, and reviewing the effectiveness of the benefits management. It also includes informing stakeholders of progress in benefits realization and assessing the performance of the changed organizational operations against performance baselines.

Progress Monitoring

Progress must be continually monitored during execution to test and assess stakeholder awareness of change (and therefore success of communications), to understand the change benefits and determine the wider change impact. This monitoring can provide an estimate of the stakeholder engagement with and support of the change.

Monitoring progress allows the change management team to report results and track the progress by individual stakeholder segments using appropriate techniques and by monitoring staff turnover, absences, tardiness, and other factors.

Effective monitoring of progress provides the necessary information for the committee of stakeholder representatives to make decisions to adjust the course of execution.

Communications with Stakeholders

The Change Management Lead should report frequently and honestly on the status of the change. This individual should describe progress in the previous period, impediments currently being encountered, and potential barriers to progress. Communications should use appropriate channels.

Stakeholder Feedback

Feedback from stakeholders provides evidence of benefits achieved to-date, those still to be achieved, and any that are no longer valid.

Benefits Realization

Achieving adoption of planned changes by impacted stakeholders is the first step toward benefits realization. Adoption of planned changes, or successfully changing the way in which people think, act, and behave to align with the future state, should result in achieving organizational outcomes (e.g., improved customer experience, improved efficiency, increased skill level of employees). When combined, these intended organizational outcomes should lead to realization of the intended benefits outlined in the business case (e.g., increased sales, cost savings, improved market share).

Executing the plan for measurement and reporting of the progress toward change readiness, adoption, achievement of organizational outcomes, and benefit realization should involve participation from the impacted business unit in order to gain input and agreement on the measurements and results. This involvement is also important in facilitating the potential transfer of accountability for measurement and reporting required for a time extending beyond the change practitioner's involvement.

Inputs	Outputs
▸ Change Management Plan ▸ Measurement and Benefit Realization Plan	▸ Measurement and Benefit Realization Reports ▸ Benefits Realization Activities

5.4.1.7 Execute Sustainability Plan

Change must be continually managed to achieve sustained results through adoption of the change and the associated values, principles, and processes. **Execute Sustainability Plan** should trigger activities and mechanisms required to cultivate a culture that will sustain the change once it has been implemented and determined to be effective and to help ensure there is not a retreat to the prior current state condition.

Activities and mechanisms should minimally include the following components:

- **Communication**: Mechanisms for persuasive communication and ongoing socialization of the change, rites of parting (saying goodbye to the old ways of doing things), and rites of enhancement (acknowledgment of quick wins and continued adoption)
- **Metrics Tracking**: Consistent and effective process for sustaining measurement and results reporting to track progress and ensure results
- **Performance Management**: Consistent process for observing and objectively measuring sustained behaviors and attitudes, including the performance appraisal process; promoting, demoting, and transferring; and learning and development
- **Rewards and Recognition:** Program of intrinsic and extrinsic incentives to sustain achieved behaviors and attitudes
- **Sustaining Ownership:** Consistent process for ensuring sustained ownership of the change through the ongoing transfer of experience and knowledge
- **Continuous Improvement:** Mechanisms for responding to changing requirements and implementing improvements based on feedback, observations, and metrics

Inputs	Outputs
▸ Sustainability Plan ▸ Measurement Baselines	▸ Communication Events ▸ Benefits Reviews ▸ Business Performance Reports ▸ Evaluations and Reviews

5.4.2 Modify the Change Management Plan as Required

The Change Management Plan will generally require modification throughout the change lifecycle in order to ensure that outcomes remain correctly aligned with the organization's needs.

Change leaders need to review objectives and make the adjustments necessary to maintain momentum and deliver results. Adjustments may include adding, eliminating, or realigning change program components to reinforce the change or decrease or accelerate change in response to internal or external pressures. Changes to deliverables should be controlled through formal procedures that are aligned with the organization's change control framework. Once a change to the Change Management Plan or Strategy has been approved, then the decision should be communicated to all relevant stakeholders.

Inputs	Outputs
▸ Change Management Plan ▸ Project Schedule and Plan	▸ Change Management Plan (updated)

5.5 Complete the Change Management Effort

The purpose of **Complete the Change Management Effort** is to document the actions and resources needed to close the change. The close effort is the point at which there is a distinct transition to maintenance or sustaining activities.

5.5.1 Evaluate the Outcome Against the Objectives

The Change Management effort should include the following actions, as required, to evaluate the outcomes against the objectives:

- Compare the outcomes of the change management effort against the change objectives set at the beginning of the change effort
- Compare the outcomes of the change management effort against project or program objectives (if project or program management is in use)
- Document the outcome of the appropriate comparisons indicating that change efforts met objectives, failed to meet objectives, or exceeded objectives
- Review outcomes with appropriate leaders/stakeholders

Inputs	Outputs
▸ Change Objectives and Goals ▸ Measurement and Benefit Realization Plan ▸ Sustainability Plan	▸ Change Objectives Analysis Outcomes and Next Steps

5.5.2 Design and Conduct Lessons Learned Evaluation and Provide Results to Establish Internal Best Practices

The purpose of conducting lessons learned is to evaluate the success or adoption outcomes of the Change Management Program, document what went well, record learnings, and share improvements for future change management programs with other change management practitioners or organizations. This step is conducted by the Change Management Lead in concert with the project manager (when possible). The final lessons learned evaluation uses the collective feedback of the team and stakeholders/customers to understand the outcome of the change management program and document improvements. It also provides a useful validation of any outstanding change management issues or activities.

Undertaking an evaluation of lessons learned reinforces the commitment of the team to continuing and sustaining the success of the change. It also enables two-way feedback regarding how the change has been embedded and future improvements for the change leads and organization.

The activities of a Lessons Learned Evaluation are to:
- Review change management activities and documents
- Identify and recognize positive outcomes and opportunities for improvement
- Develop a Remediation Plan for change management activities to address key issues
- Verify and document actions for future projects
- Document lessons learned in a knowledge management database or common document storage location for sharing with other change management practitioners

Identify Appropriate Group to Conduct Evaluation

Key individuals and groups affected can be identified for participation using the outputs delivered. The Change Management Lead conducts an evaluation of lessons learned by bringing together team members, key stakeholders, the project sponsor, leadership, affected staff/customers, and other appropriate parties.

Perform the Lessons Learned Evaluation

The purpose of bringing key individuals together during this process is to:
- Review the change management objectives
- Review each phase and its key objectives
- Review the effectiveness of each change management workstream against its key objectives and defined outcomes
- Review the effectiveness of the approach and ways of working
- Verify that the change management goals of the initiative were reached and validate key change actions for future projects
- Identify good outcomes and points for improvement, including any possible mitigation or improvement based on the current initiative
- Review change management activities and documents for other best practices or future improvements
- Determine which designs, strategies, and lessons learned will contribute to internal best practices going forward
- Update the knowledge management database or common document storage location for sharing the lessons learned with other change management practitioners

The Change Management Lead produces a document that presents lessons learned in a logical manner. The document should provide guidance and best practices for future change initiatives.

The Lessons Learned Evaluation document should consider questions such as:
- What are repeatable, successful activities?
- How can we ensure future projects go as well or better?
- What advice would you give to future teams?
- What are some individual successes?

Inputs	Outputs
▸ Case for Change ▸ Success Criteria and Measures ▸ Change Management Plan	▸ Lessons Learned Evaluation ▸ Remediation Plan

5.5.3 Gain Approval for Completion, Transfer of Ownership, and Release of Resources

Several activities need to be completed during this final step to formally close the change.

Gain Approval for Completion

Approval should be sought from the stakeholder steering committee, senior sponsor, or client confirming that the closure conditions have been met, including:

- An evaluation of outcomes against objectives according to the agreed scope of the change
- A report of the lessons learned through the change
- A document demonstrating the transfer of the change outcomes to the appropriate stakeholder operational owners
- A plan to release any remaining change resources

Transfer Ownership

The ownership of all change outcomes (processes, technology, organizations, and other outcomes) must be transferred from change resources to stakeholder operational resources. This should be evidenced by written agreement of both parties. Additionally, transfer of future strategy plans must also occur if part of the outcomes.

Release of Resources

All change resources should be released and made available for use in other change efforts.

Inputs	Outputs
▸ Change Objectives and Goals ▸ Measurement and Benefit Realization Plan ▸ Lessons Learned Report ▸ Future Strategy Plan ▸ Agreement on Ownership Transfer ▸ Resource Release Approval	▸ Final Summary Report ▸ Change Initiative Completion

Appendix A: ACMP Statement of Change Management

Introduction

The Association of Change Management Professionals® (ACMP) is a global membership organization whose purpose is to advance the discipline of change management. ACMP provides:

1. A structured environment to facilitate change management as a professional discipline.
2. A professional recognition and certification program for change management practitioners.
3. Opportunities for professional growth, networking, and learning.
4. A globally recognized standard of generally accepted and effective change management norms, practices, and processes.
5. Identification of new trends, needs, and opportunities to advance the field.

In order to fulfill its purposes, ACMP develops and promotes a common definition and understanding of the discipline of change management. This includes a common lexicon; the knowledge, skills, and abilities expected of a professional change management practitioner; and the processes and practices that apply to most change management implementations.

This document provides the boundary conditions for ACMP's Change Management Certification programs and serves as a guiding framework for the development of a change management standard. ACMP recognizes change management as a professional discipline and provides standards and certification to support professionals in this field.

Change Management Definition

ACMP defines change management as the application of knowledge, skills, abilities, methodologies, processes, tools, and techniques to transition an individual or group from a current state to a future state to achieve expected benefits and organizational objectives. Change management processes, when properly applied, ensure individuals within an organization efficiently and effectively transition through change so that the organization's goals are realized. Change management is an integral part of the overall change process and ideally begins at the onset of change. ACMP's definition assumes that the organization has agreed upon the need for change and has identified the nature of the change.

Scope and Boundaries

ACMP's change management standard will overlap with other professional disciplines that may have their own standards and certification. Effective change agents will need strong leadership skills, interpersonal skills, emotional intelligence, and excellent verbal and written communication skills. They will need to navigate complex political environments, operate within various geographic and organizational cultures, work at multiple levels within an organization, and engage many different types of personalities in the workplace.

Change management professionals need a broad set of knowledge and skills to enable them to be effective change managers and change consultants. However, any attempt to create a standard and certification program that addresses all of these knowledge and skills areas would be problematic in scope and subjective in implementation. Therefore, ACMP will create an objective and measurable standard for the application of change management as a professional discipline but will not certify the relative effectiveness of a "person" as a change manager or change consultant. This distinction enables the creation of a change management standard and certification program with the following characteristics:

1. ACMP's change management standard will have defined boundaries.

2. ACMP's change management standard will not overlap with other professional disciplines, which may have their own standards and certification.

3. ACMP's change management standard will have objective and measurable performance criteria.

The net result of this distinction between certifying a person as an "effective change manager" versus certifying in the practice of change management is that some knowledge and skill areas of an effective change manager will be out of scope for ACMP's certification and standards process, at least for the initial development of Level 1 and Level 2 certifications. For example, ACMP will not develop standards and certification for general leadership competencies, cross-cultural competencies, interpersonal skills, or consultative skills. ACMP may examine these broader knowledge and skill areas in terms of their impact on effective change management at a future time.

ACMP also recognizes that change management is a complementary discipline to other professional disciplines that work together to bring about change. For example, changes in organizations may affect stakeholders' work processes, software applications, systems, tools, organizational structures, job descriptions, work locations, or overall work environment. Each type of change requires different professional disciplines to develop the technical element of the change, including hardware development, software development, organizational structure design, job role design, strategy development, and process and workflow design.

The professional disciplines that create the technical elements of the change are necessary and complementary disciplines to change management but are out of scope for ACMP standards and certification work. For example, ACMP will not develop standards and certification for areas such as vision and strategy development, new product/service offerings, process design and improvement, organizational design, job role design, hardware/software/equipment development, or system testing. Similarly, the structured management of the resources, deliverables, and schedule for the change process, often referred to as project management, is a complementary discipline to change management. ACMP will not be developing standards and certification for project management.

ACMP recognizes that knowledge, skills, and abilities in the table below are unique and critical to the discipline of change management and are therefore within the scope of its recognition and certification programs.

Knowledge and Skill Areas	Description and Examples
The process of change	Change drivers, the change process, overall context for how change happens in organizations, change leadership and project governance, mechanisms for creating the "content" of the change, patterns of change success and failures, emotional components of the change process for individuals
Change management vocabulary	Terms and definitions, general framework, and context
Change management methodologies and tools	Processes and tools for change management
Relationship and integration of change management with other disciplines	Integration with project management, integration with other business improvement methodologies such as Six Sigma, Lean
Change management strategy, architecture, and planning	Change management architecture, strategy development, change management planning, impact and risk assessments
Change management team structures	Leadership alignment, roles/responsibilities, budget, resources, team preparation, governance, subject matter expertise
Change leader/sponsor development	Change leader/sponsor education, sponsor skill and willingness, sponsor effectiveness assessments, sponsor coalition analysis, creating alignment among sponsors and senior leaders, change leadership/sponsor coaching, reporting and updates for sponsors
Organizational and culture assessments	Culture assessments, change impact assessments, change readiness assessments, change saturation assessments, organization and change history assessments, resistance assessments, stakeholder readiness assessments
Stakeholder engagement	Stakeholder analysis, planning, implementation, and sustainability as needed to support a change
Communications in support of the change process	Communication strategy, planning, and communication activities as needed to support a change
Training in support of the change process	Training strategy, requirements, planning, and training activities as needed to support a change
Leading stakeholders through change	Coaching of stakeholders through change by supervisors and managers to enable successful individual transitions
Stakeholder engagement	Feedback, performance measurement, and compliance with new job roles, responsibilities, systems, and processes
Resistance management	Resistance identification and management techniques to support a change, building commitment and acceptance, risk management
Organizational change competency	Developing organizational competencies and capacity to change, continuous improvement of the change process, cultural shifts
Change performance measurement	Success measures, monitoring progress, sustaining the change

Appendix B: Process Groups Mapped to Subject Groups

The following figures illustrate the interactions of the individual processes in the five process groups identified in **5 Change Management Process** mapped to the subject groups. The interactions illustrated represent only one possible view of the processes. The arrows do not necessarily represent a sequence of processes. The change management practitioner decides which processes are required and their sequence. Any process may be repeated.

The first five figures map the processes within each process group based upon their subject group. The remaining figures map the processes within each subject group based upon the process groups.

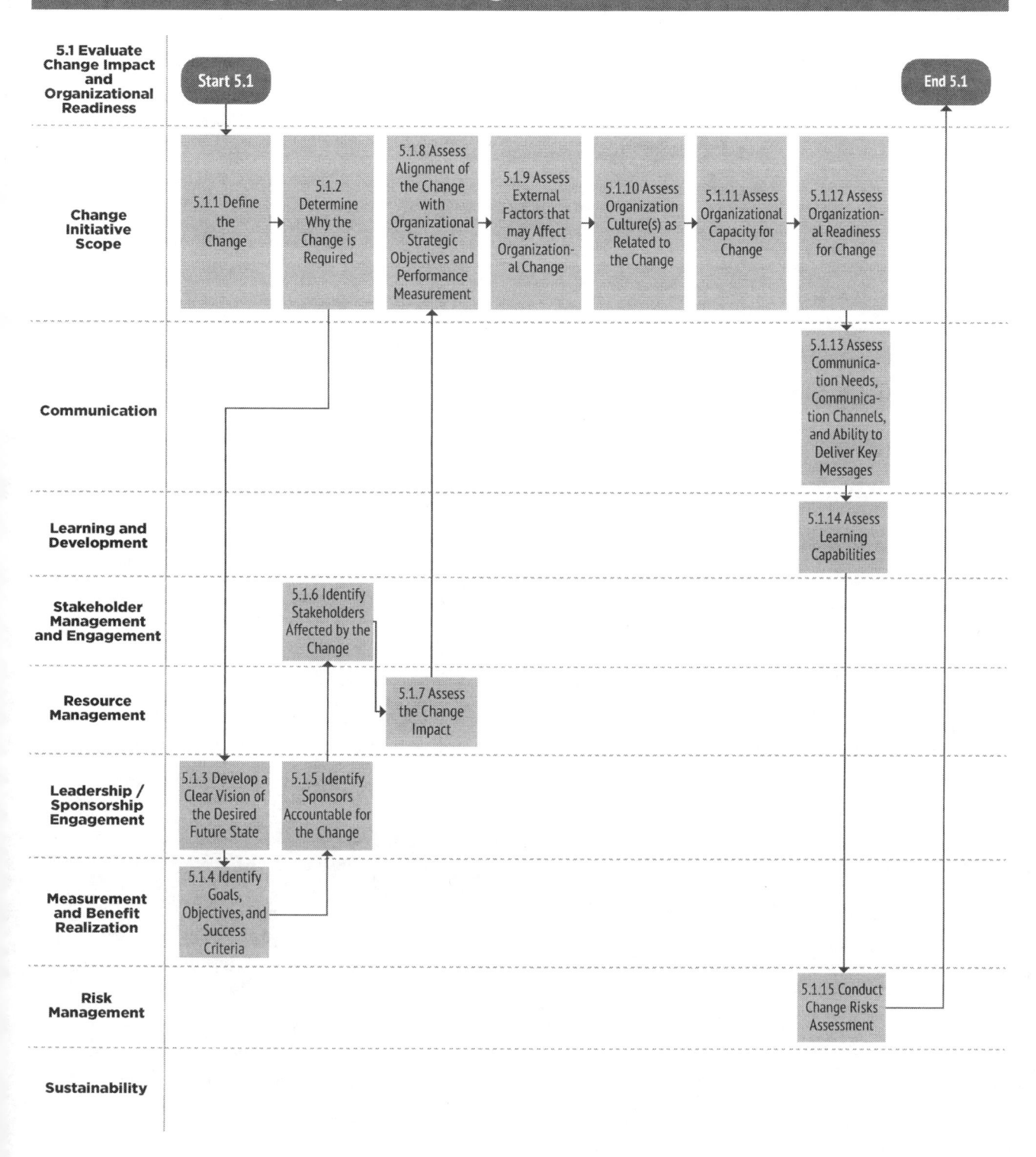

Standard for Change Management©

5.1 Evaluate Change Impact and Organizational Readiness

5.1 Evaluate Change Impact and Organizational Readiness

Start 5.1 → End 5.1

Change Initiative Scope
- 5.1.1 Define the Change
- 5.1.2 Determine Why the Change is Required
- 5.1.8 Assess Alignment of the Change with Organizational Strategic Objectives and Performance Measurement
- 5.1.9 Assess External Factors that may Affect Organizational Change
- 5.1.10 Assess Organization Culture(s) as Related to the Change
- 5.1.11 Assess Organizational Capacity for Change
- 5.1.12 Assess Organizational Readiness for Change

Communication
- 5.1.13 Assess Communication Needs, Communication Channels, and Ability to Deliver Key Messages

Learning and Development
- 5.1.14 Assess Learning Capabilities

Stakeholder Management and Engagement
- 5.1.6 Identify Stakeholders Affected by the Change

Resource Management
- 5.1.7 Assess the Change Impact

Leadership / Sponsorship Engagement
- 5.1.3 Develop a Clear Vision of the Desired Future State
- 5.1.5 Identify Sponsors Accountable for the Change

Measurement and Benefit Realization
- 5.1.4 Identify Goals, Objectives, and Success Criteria

Risk Management
- 5.1.15 Conduct Change Risks Assessment

Sustainability

Copyright © 2019 Association of Change Management Professionals® (ACMP®) All Rights Reserved

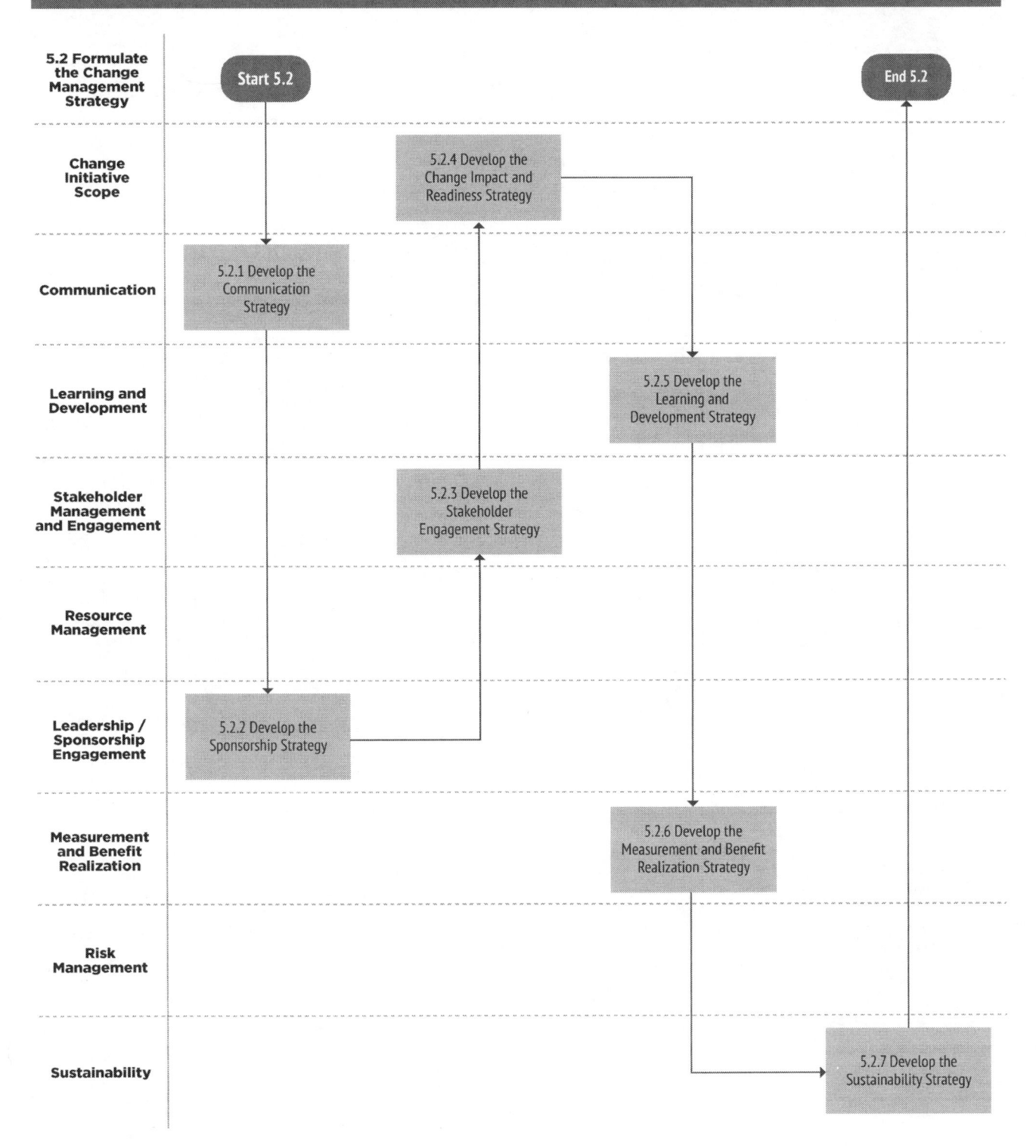

5.2 Formulate the Change Management Strategy

Swimlane	Activities
5.2 Formulate the Change Management Strategy	Start 5.2 → ... → End 5.2
Change Initiative Scope	5.2.4 Develop the Change Impact and Readiness Strategy
Communication	5.2.1 Develop the Communication Strategy
Learning and Development	5.2.5 Develop the Learning and Development Strategy
Stakeholder Management and Engagement	5.2.3 Develop the Stakeholder Engagement Strategy
Resource Management	
Leadership / Sponsorship Engagement	5.2.2 Develop the Sponsorship Strategy
Measurement and Benefit Realization	5.2.6 Develop the Measurement and Benefit Realization Strategy
Risk Management	
Sustainability	5.2.7 Develop the Sustainability Strategy

Flow: Start 5.2 → 5.2.1 Develop the Communication Strategy → 5.2.2 Develop the Sponsorship Strategy → 5.2.3 Develop the Stakeholder Engagement Strategy → 5.2.4 Develop the Change Impact and Readiness Strategy → 5.2.5 Develop the Learning and Development Strategy → 5.2.6 Develop the Measurement and Benefit Realization Strategy → 5.2.7 Develop the Sustainability Strategy → End 5.2

Copyright © 2019 Association of Change Management Professionals® (ACMP®) All Rights Reserved

5.3 Develop the Change Management Plan

5.3 Develop the Change Management Plan

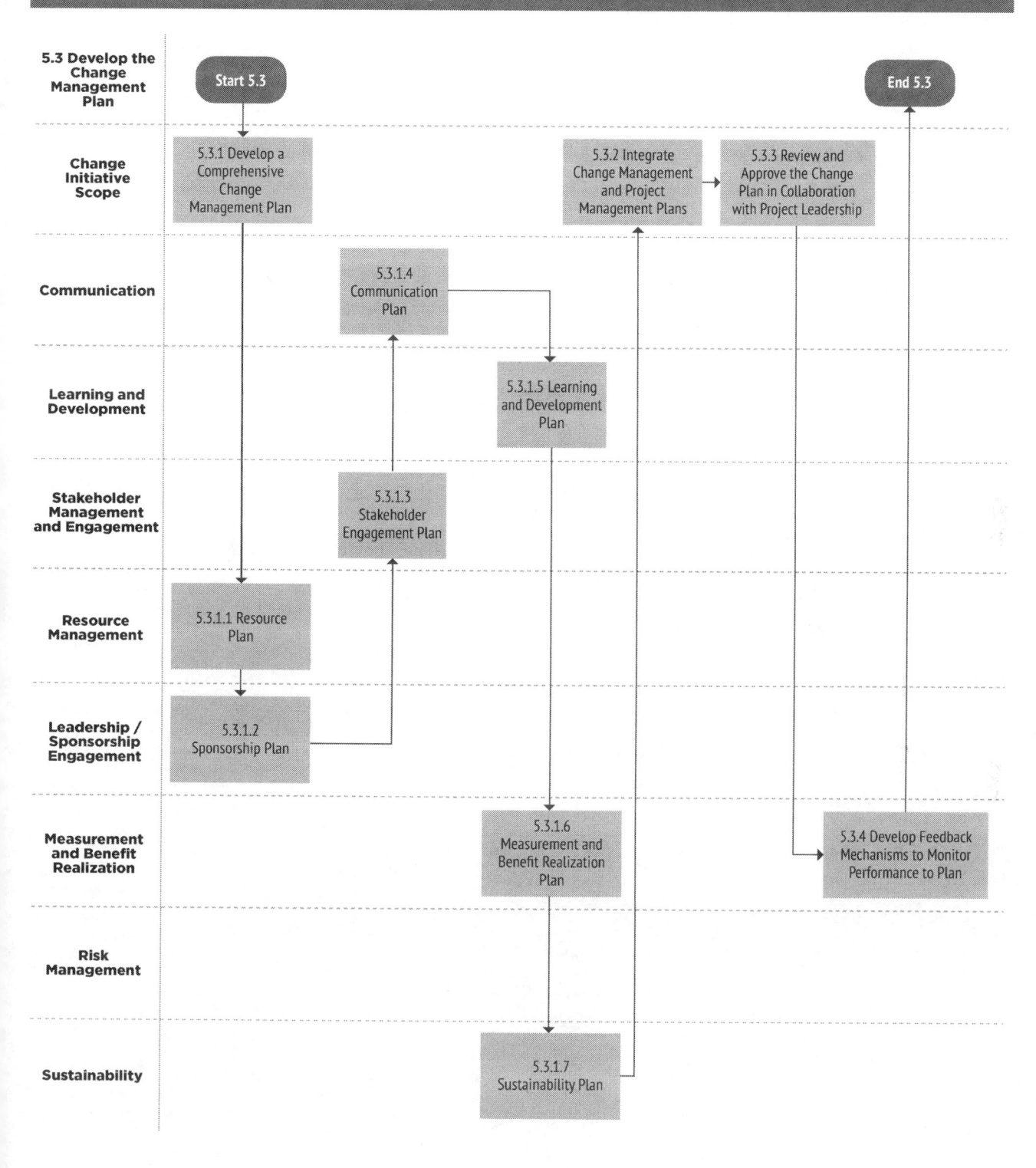

- Start 5.3 → 5.3.1 Develop a Comprehensive Change Management Plan
- End 5.3

Change Initiative Scope
- 5.3.1 Develop a Comprehensive Change Management Plan
- 5.3.2 Integrate Change Management and Project Management Plans
- 5.3.3 Review and Approve the Change Plan in Collaboration with Project Leadership

Communication
- 5.3.1.4 Communication Plan

Learning and Development
- 5.3.1.5 Learning and Development Plan

Stakeholder Management and Engagement
- 5.3.1.3 Stakeholder Engagement Plan

Resource Management
- 5.3.1.1 Resource Plan

Leadership / Sponsorship Engagement
- 5.3.1.2 Sponsorship Plan

Measurement and Benefit Realization
- 5.3.1.6 Measurement and Benefit Realization Plan
- 5.3.4 Develop Feedback Mechanisms to Monitor Performance to Plan

Risk Management

Sustainability
- 5.3.1.7 Sustainability Plan

Standard for Change Management©

Copyright © 2019 Association of Change Management Professionals® (ACMP®) All Rights Reserved

5.4 Execute the Change Management Plan

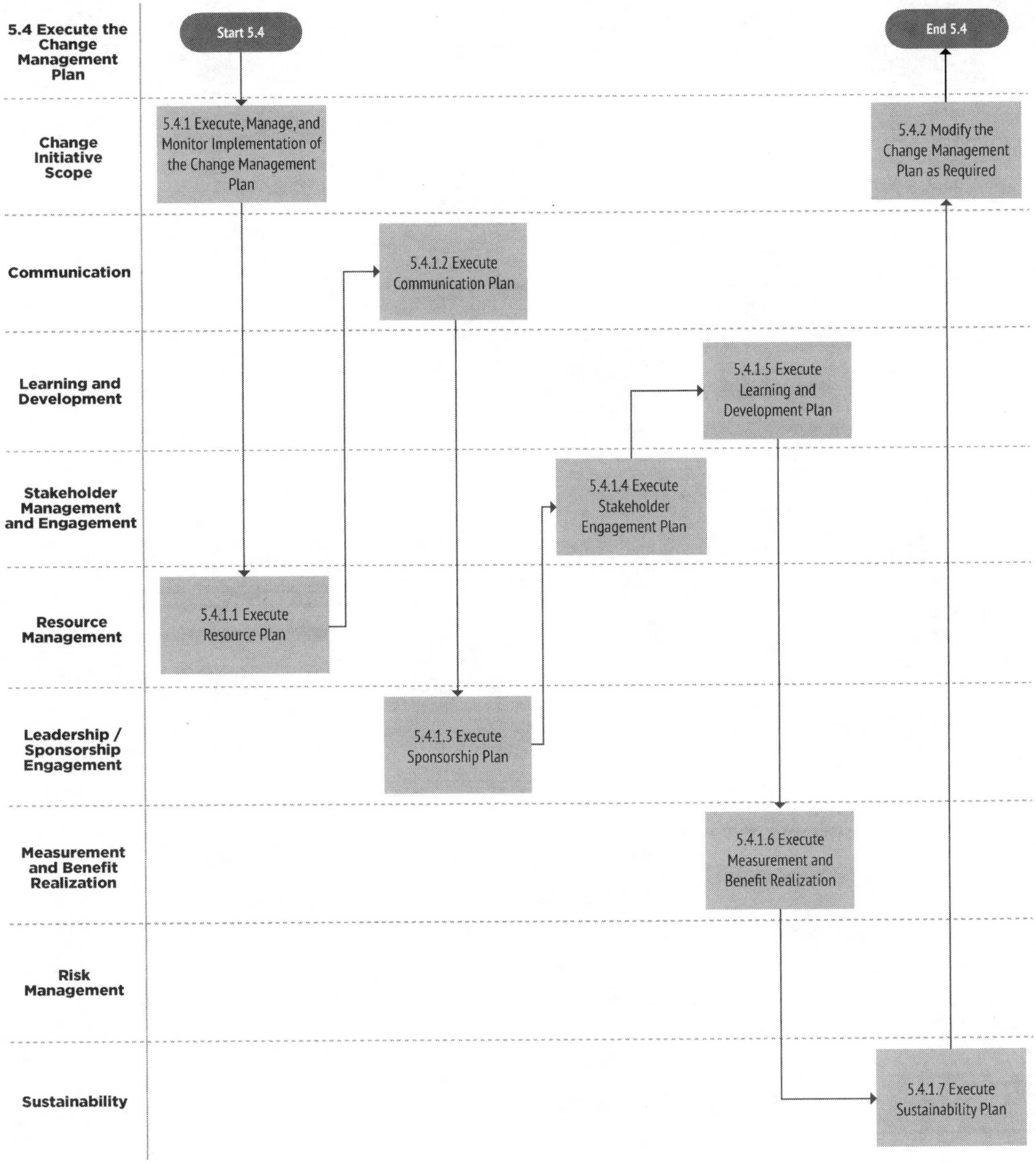
5.4 Execute the Change Management Plan
Start 5.4
End 5.4
Change Initiative Scope
5.4.1 Execute, Manage, and Monitor Implementation of the Change Management Plan
5.4.2 Modify the Change Management Plan as Required
Communication
5.4.1.2 Execute Communication Plan
Learning and Development
5.4.1.5 Execute Learning and Development Plan
Stakeholder Management and Engagement
5.4.1.4 Execute Stakeholder Engagement Plan
Resource Management
5.4.1.1 Execute Resource Plan
Leadership / Sponsorship Engagement
5.4.1.3 Execute Sponsorship Plan
Measurement and Benefit Realization
5.4.1.6 Execute Measurement and Benefit Realization
Risk Management
Sustainability
5.4.1.7 Execute Sustainability Plan

Copyright © 2019 Association of Change Management Professionals® (ACMP®) All Rights Reserved

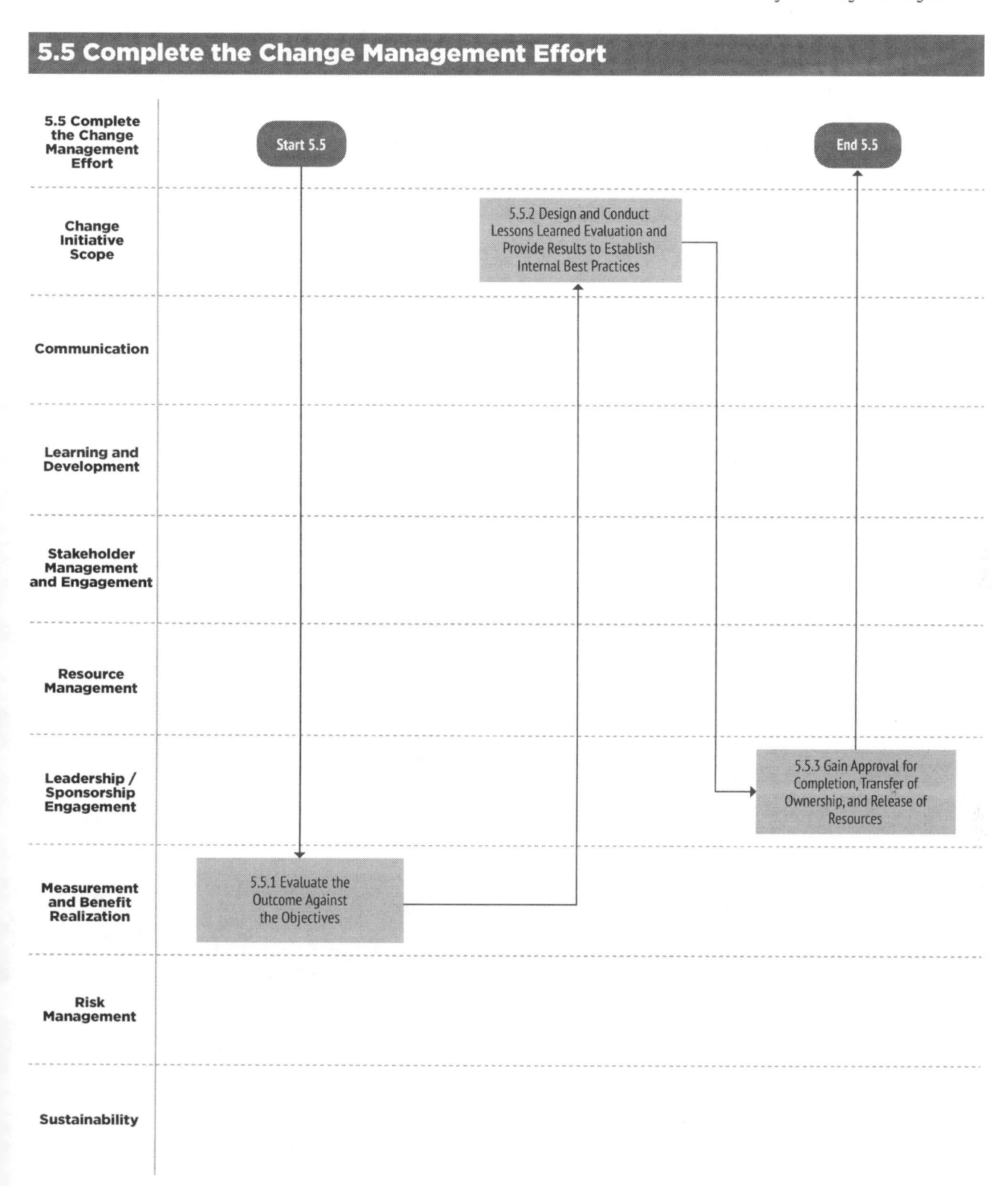

Standard for Change Management©

5.5 Complete the Change Management Effort

5.5 Complete the Change Management Effort	Start 5.5 → End 5.5
Change Initiative Scope	5.5.2 Design and Conduct Lessons Learned Evaluation and Provide Results to Establish Internal Best Practices
Communication	
Learning and Development	
Stakeholder Management and Engagement	
Resource Management	
Leadership / Sponsorship Engagement	5.5.3 Gain Approval for Completion, Transfer of Ownership, and Release of Resources
Measurement and Benefit Realization	5.5.1 Evaluate the Outcome Against the Objectives
Risk Management	
Sustainability	

Copyright © 2019 Association of Change Management Professionals® (ACMP®) All Rights Reserved

Standard for Change Management©

Change Initiative Scope

5.1 Evaluate Change Impact and Organizational Readiness	5.2 Formulate Change Management Strategy	5.3 Develop the Change Management Plan	5.4 Execute the Change Management Plan	5.5 Complete the Change Management Effort

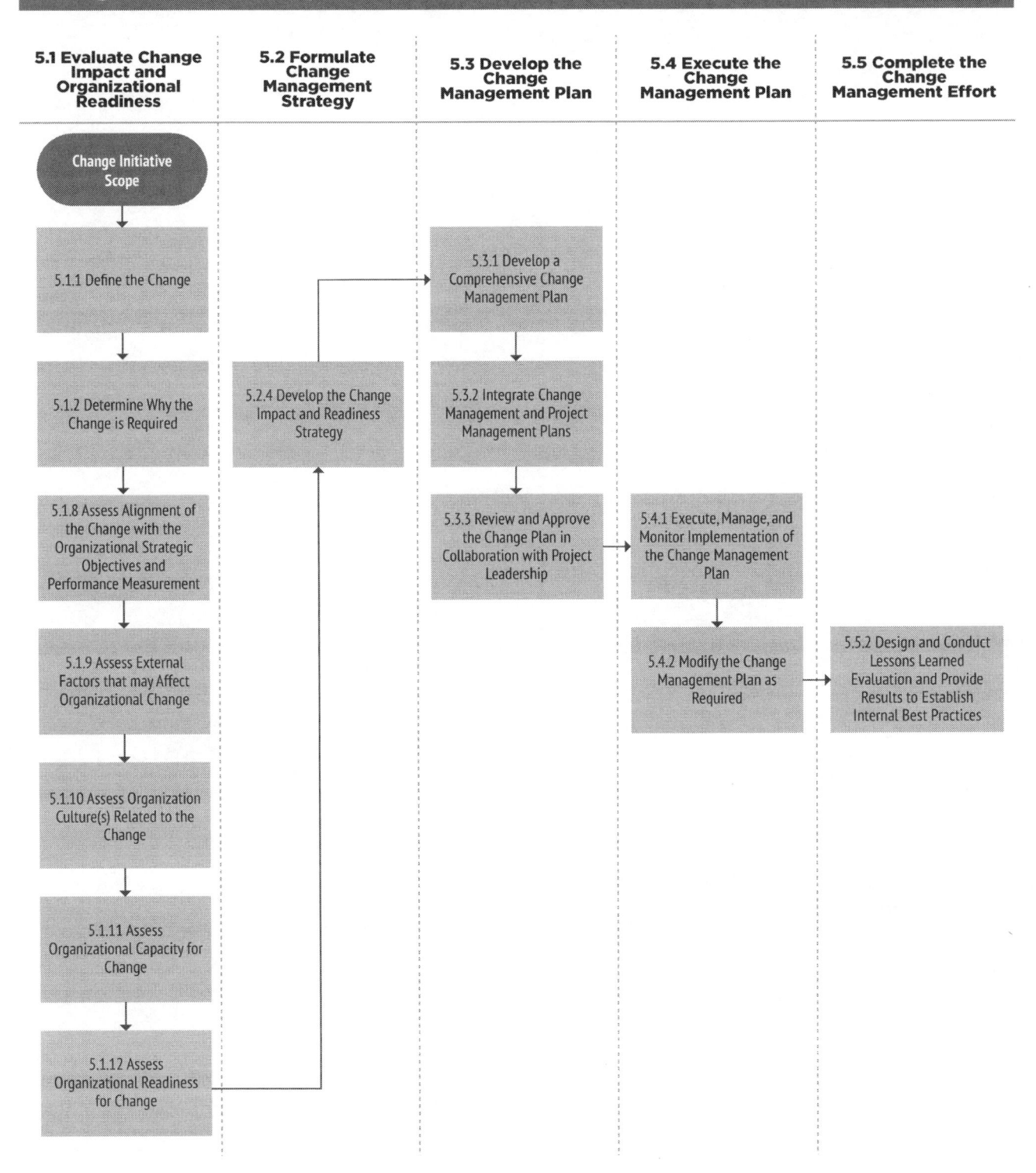

Change Initiative Scope

↓

5.1.1 Define the Change

↓

5.1.2 Determine Why the Change is Required

↓

5.1.8 Assess Alignment of the Change with the Organizational Strategic Objectives and Performance Measurement

↓

5.1.9 Assess External Factors that may Affect Organizational Change

↓

5.1.10 Assess Organization Culture(s) Related to the Change

↓

5.1.11 Assess Organizational Capacity for Change

↓

5.1.12 Assess Organizational Readiness for Change

→ 5.2.4 Develop the Change Impact and Readiness Strategy

→ 5.3.1 Develop a Comprehensive Change Management Plan

↓

5.3.2 Integrate Change Management and Project Management Plans

↓

5.3.3 Review and Approve the Change Plan in Collaboration with Project Leadership

→ 5.4.1 Execute, Manage, and Monitor Implementation of the Change Management Plan

↓

5.4.2 Modify the Change Management Plan as Required

→ 5.5.2 Design and Conduct Lessons Learned Evaluation and Provide Results to Establish Internal Best Practices

Copyright © 2019 Association of Change Management Professionals® (ACMP®) All Rights Reserved

Standard for Change Management©

Communication

5.1 Evaluate Change Impact and Organizational Readiness	5.2 Formulate Change Management Strategy	5.3 Develop the Change Management Plan	5.4 Execute the Change Management Plan	5.5 Complete the Change Management Effort
Communication				
5.1.13 Assess Communication Needs, Communication Channels, and Ability to Deliver Key Messages	5.2.1 Develop the Communication Strategy	5.3.1.2 Sponsorship Plan	5.4.1.2 Execute the Communication Plan	

Leadership/Sponsorship Engagement

5.1 Evaluate Change Impact and Organizational Readiness	5.2 Formulate Change Management Strategy	5.3 Develop the Change Management Plan	5.4 Execute the Change Management Plan	5.5 Complete the Change Management Effort
Leadership / Sponsorship Engagement				
5.1.3 Develop a Clear Vision of the Desired Future State		5.3.1.3 Stakeholder Engagement Plan		
	5.2.2 Develop the Sponsorship Strategy			
5.1.5 Identify Sponsors Accountable for the Change			5.4.1.3 Execute the Sponsorship Plan	5.5.3 Gain Approval for Completion, Transfer of Ownership, and Release of Resources

Copyright © 2019 Association of Change Management Professionals® (ACMP®) All Rights Reserved

Standard for Change Management

Learning and Development

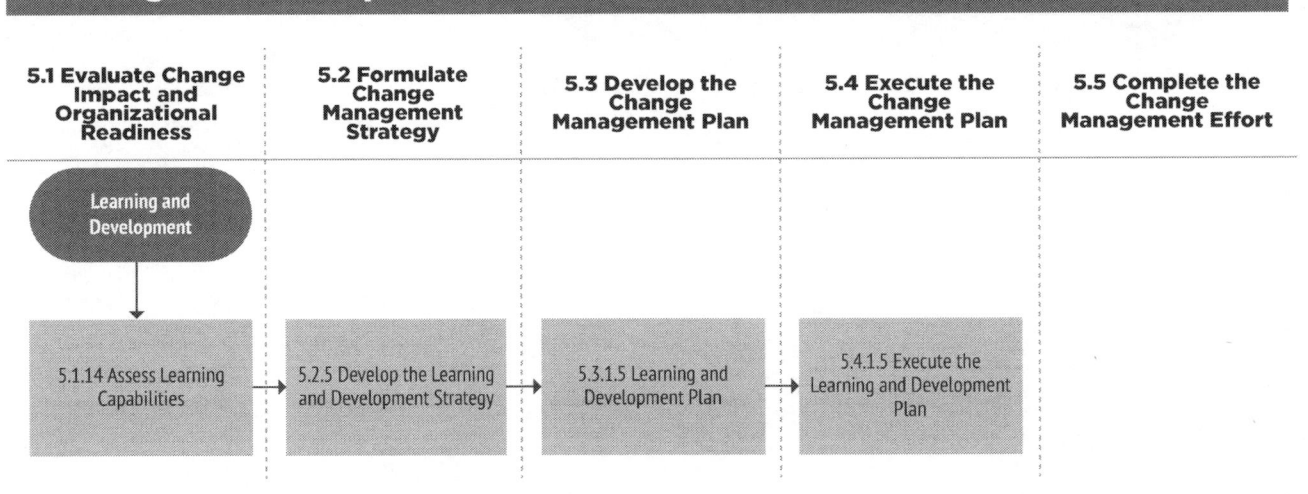

5.1 Evaluate Change Impact and Organizational Readiness	5.2 Formulate Change Management Strategy	5.3 Develop the Change Management Plan	5.4 Execute the Change Management Plan	5.5 Complete the Change Management Effort
Learning and Development				
5.1.14 Assess Learning Capabilities	5.2.5 Develop the Learning and Development Strategy	5.3.1.5 Learning and Development Plan	5.4.1.5 Execute the Learning and Development Plan	

Measurement and Benefit Realization

5.1 Evaluate Change Impact and Organizational Readiness	5.2 Formulate Change Management Strategy	5.3 Develop the Change Management Plan	5.4 Execute the Change Management Plan	5.5 Complete the Change Management Effort
Measurement and Benefit Realization				
5.1.4 Identify Goals, Objectives, and Success Criteria	5.2.6 Develop the Measurement and Benefit Realization Strategy	5.3.1.6 Measurement and Benefit Realization Plan	5.4.1.6 Execute the Measurement and Benefit Realization Plan	5.5.1 Evaluate the Outcome Against the Objectives
		5.3.4 Develop Feedback Mechanisms to Monitor Performance to Plan		

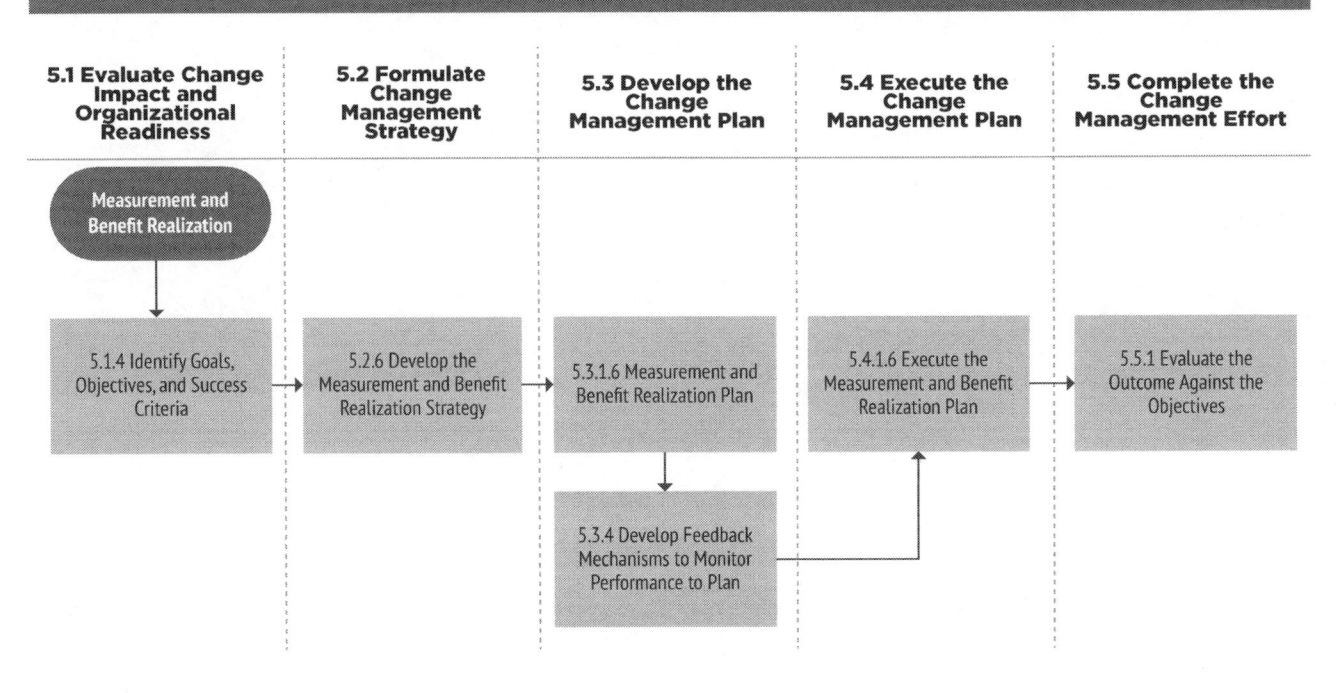

Copyright © 2019 Association of Change Management Professionals® (ACMP®) All Rights Reserved

Standard for Change Management©

Resource Management

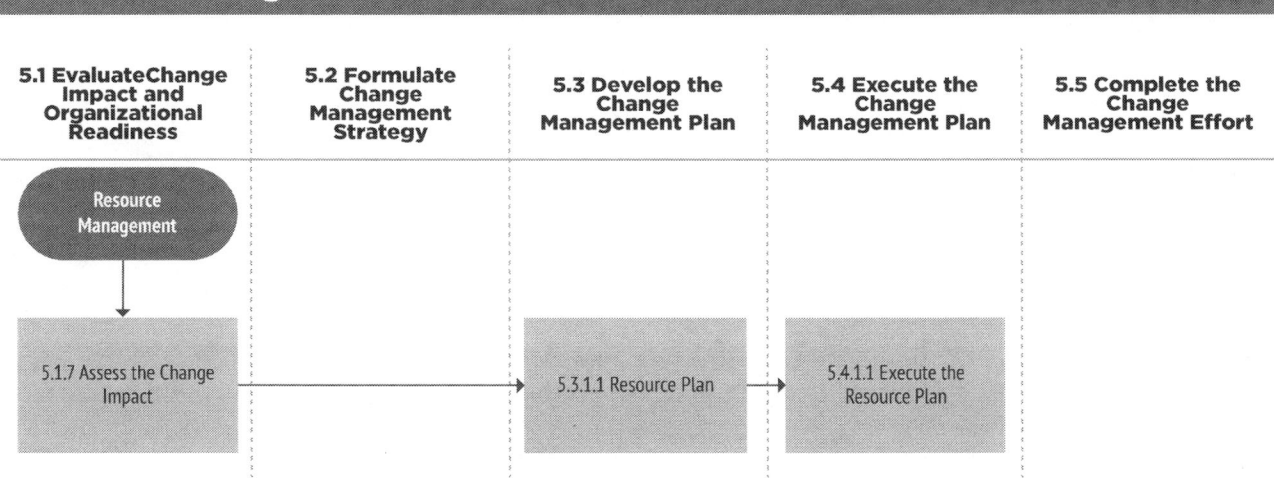

5.1 Evaluate Change Impact and Organizational Readiness	5.2 Formulate Change Management Strategy	5.3 Develop the Change Management Plan	5.4 Execute the Change Management Plan	5.5 Complete the Change Management Effort
Resource Management → 5.1.7 Assess the Change Impact		5.3.1.1 Resource Plan	5.4.1.1 Execute the Resource Plan	

Risk Management

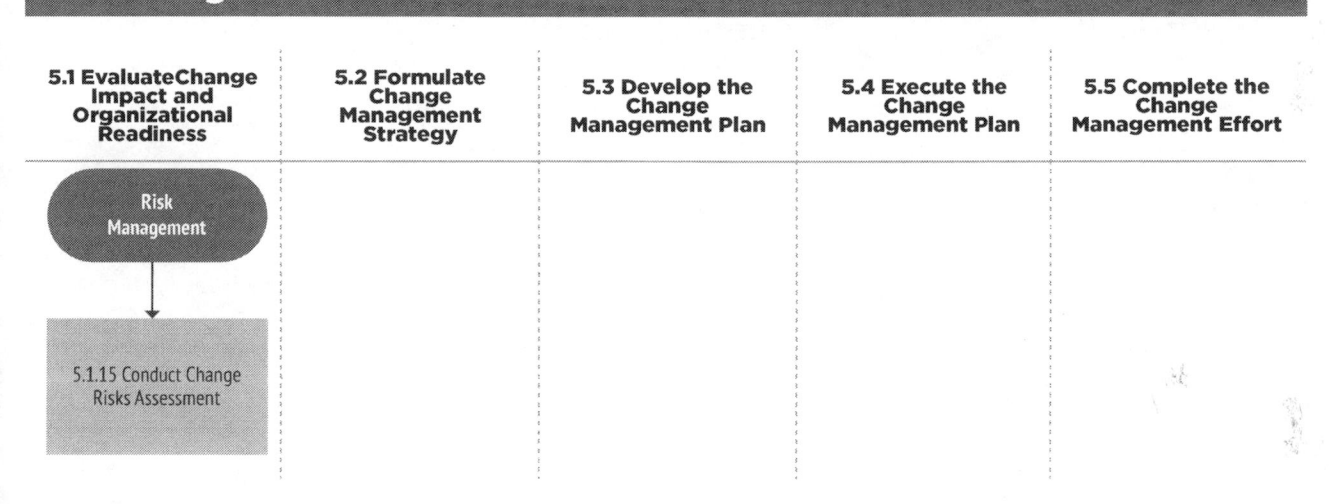

5.1 Evaluate Change Impact and Organizational Readiness	5.2 Formulate Change Management Strategy	5.3 Develop the Change Management Plan	5.4 Execute the Change Management Plan	5.5 Complete the Change Management Effort
Risk Management → 5.1.15 Conduct Change Risks Assessment				

Copyright © 2019 Association of Change Management Professionals® (ACMP®) All Rights Reserved

Standard for Change Management©

Stakeholder Management and Engagement

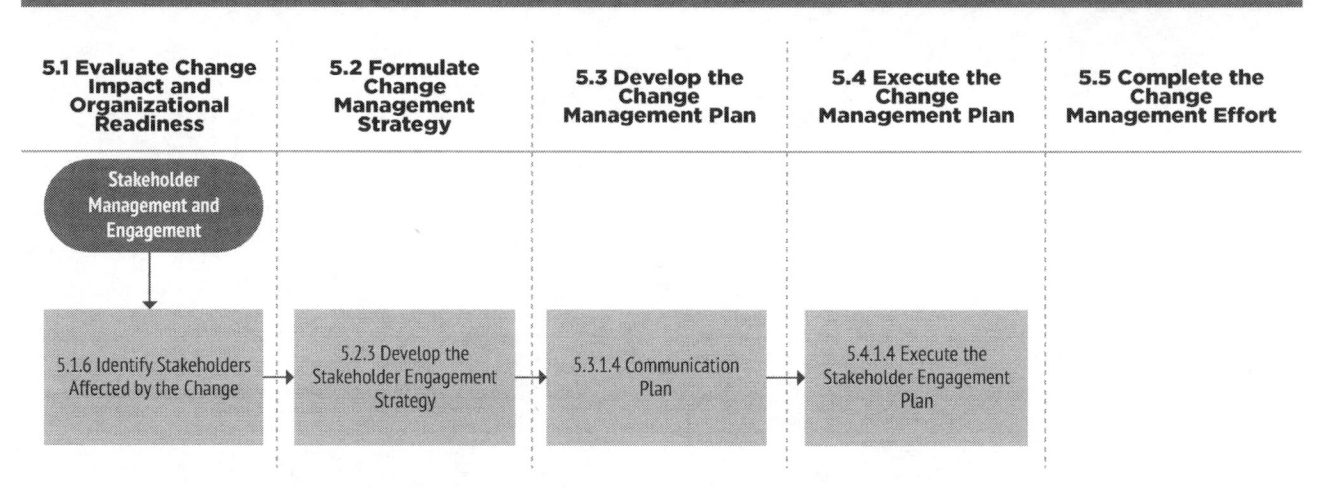

5.1 Evaluate Change Impact and Organizational Readiness	5.2 Formulate Change Management Strategy	5.3 Develop the Change Management Plan	5.4 Execute the Change Management Plan	5.5 Complete the Change Management Effort
Stakeholder Management and Engagement ↓				
5.1.6 Identify Stakeholders Affected by the Change	5.2.3 Develop the Stakeholder Engagement Strategy	5.3.1.4 Communication Plan	5.4.1.4 Execute the Stakeholder Engagement Plan	

Sustainability

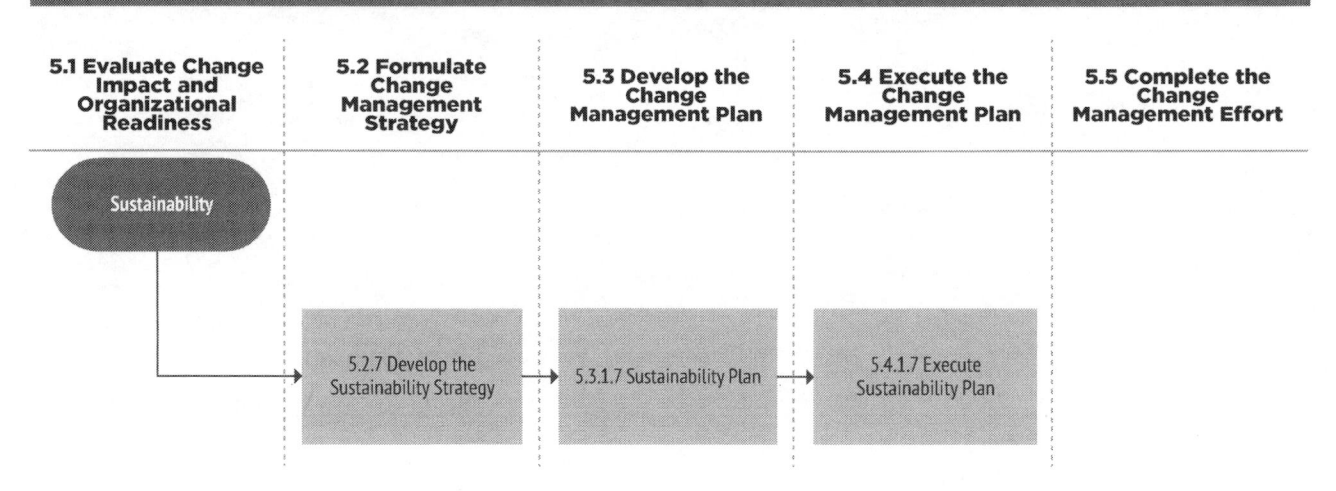

5.1 Evaluate Change Impact and Organizational Readiness	5.2 Formulate Change Management Strategy	5.3 Develop the Change Management Plan	5.4 Execute the Change Management Plan	5.5 Complete the Change Management Effort
Sustainability ↓				
	5.2.7 Develop the Sustainability Strategy	5.3.1.7 Sustainability Plan	5.4.1.7 Execute Sustainability Plan	

Copyright © 2019 Association of Change Management Professionals® (ACMP®) All Rights Reserved

Part II:
ACMP Change Management Code of Ethics

Alignment to ACMP's Vision

When the Association of Change Management Professionals (ACMP) launched in 2011, it represented a significant milestone in the field of Change Management. Other Change Management organizations can rightly claim specific areas of expertise, such as defining best practices supported through research, delivering knowledge and skills through training programs, creating unique methodologies which help shape strategy and execution, and providing quality consulting services. ACMP fills an equally important but complementary role, providing practitioners a professional association devoted to helping them to advance the discipline and increase change effectiveness around the world.

There are three required components in order to be considered a profession: the development of a unique set of professional standards, the creation and maintenance of a certification process, and the establishment of guidelines which govern the profession as a whole. Each is equally important, and ACMP cannot exist successfully without all three. To help guide the profession, ACMP has adopted the Change Management Professional Code of Ethics, which articulates the minimum expectations for professional conduct for Change Management practitioners. It establishes guidelines for responsible behavior and sets forth a common understanding for how to identify and resolve ethical dilemmas.

I. Purpose of ACMP's Code of Ethics

The purpose of this Code of Ethics is to guide the professional conduct of members of the association, holders and applicants of ACMP-sponsored certifications, volunteers, ACMP Qualified Training Providers, staff, and contracted resources. This document addresses specific professional conduct for every individual bound by this Code.

II. Alignment of ACMP's Ethics to the Change Management Standard

The ultimate goal of ACMP's Code of Ethics is to outline and communicate minimum professional expectations to change practitioners. The tenets defined in this document support and complement the more specific behaviors and guidelines defined in ACMP's Standard document.

III. Scope of Coverage

The Code of Ethics applies to the following individuals:

a. ACMP Members

b. ACMP Certificate Holders and Applicants

c. ACMP volunteers, staff, and contractors

d. ACMP Qualified Education Providers™ (QEPTM)

Structure of the Code

The ACMP Code of Ethics is divided into sections that contain tenets of conduct outlined within five duties identified as most important to the global change management community. These duties include: Honesty, Responsibility, Fairness, Respect, and Advancing the Discipline and Supporting Practitioners. This Code affirms these duties as the foundation for ethical and professional behavior for change management practitioners governed by this document. Descriptions and examples cited throughout this document are not intended to be prescriptive, but are instead included to provide practical illustrations of change management professionalism.

Mandatory Conduct

ACMP's Code of Ethics is intended to promote ethical practices in the profession. Change management professionals are responsible for adding value to the organizations they serve and ethically contributing to the success of those organizations. Change practitioners accept personal responsibility for their decisions and actions. Each section of the Code of Ethics includes mandatory tenets that establish firm requirements, and in some cases, limit or prohibit specific behaviors. Practitioners who do not conduct themselves in accordance with these tenets may be subject to disciplinary procedures.

IV. ACMP Ethical Standards

4.1 Duty of Honesty

Honesty is central to ethical behavior and ACMP's values. Our duty is to demonstrate honesty through understanding the truth and acting in a truthful manner both in our communications and in our conduct.

Honesty in Communications

As practitioners in the global change management community we demonstrate honesty in communications, conduct, and through our behavior in three significant dimensions by:

ACMP Change Management Code of Ethics

Truth
- Earnestly seeking to understand the truth
- Knowingly communicating with intent to express truth, ensuring that due diligence is undertaken to extract truth at every opportunity
- Expressing truth in our communications in a way that is not likely to deceive or mislead
- Providing accurate information in a timely manner

Sincerity
- Acting with sincerity, communicating genuinely, and ensuring meaningful expression of intent
- Making commitments and promises, implied or explicit, in good faith
- Striving to create an environment in which others feel safe to tell the truth

Candor
- Establishing relationships with legitimate expectations of frank, forthright exchanges based on mutual trust
- Seeking to conduct all exchanges with others respectfully, emphasizing openness and frank discussion as critical to healthy communication

Honesty in Conduct and Behavior

As practitioners in the global change management community, we demonstrate honesty in conduct and behavior by:

- Conducting ourselves always in a manner that consistently demonstrates our integrity
- Engaging in honest behavior with the intention of preserving the interity of self, the client or employer we represent and all other staff members
- Engaging in behavior that demonstrates our consistent trustworthiness, acting on our core values in decision making with assured expectation and reliability
- Acting consistently regardless of the situation, remaining dutiful in representing our personal and professional ethics through behavior and word assuming full responsibility for our own actions

4.2 Duty of Responsibility

Ethical responsibility is demonstrated through accountability while pursuing excellence and responding to expectations. Responsibility implies that we take full ownership for the decisions we make or fail to make, the actions we take or fail to take, and the consequences that result.

As practitioners in the global change management community we demonstrate duty of responsibility by:

- Making decisions and taking actions based on the best interests of society, public safety, and the environment
- Accepting only those assignments that are consistent with our background, experience, skills, and qualifications
- Competently and completely fulfilling the commitments that we undertake – we do what we say we will do
- Taking ownership of our errors or omissions and the resulting consequences, ensuring that communication to the appropriate body occurs. and that we make corrections promptly

Copyright © 2019 Association of Change Management Professionals® (ACMP®) All Rights Reserved

ACMP Change Management Code of Ethics

- Promptly communicating to the appropriate body any errors or omissions discovered that are caused by others
- Protecting proprietary or confidential information that has been entrusted to us
- Ensuring that key stakeholders are completely informed if developmental or stretch assignments being considered exceed our qualifications or skills thereby enabling our client/employer/co-workers to make informed decisions for our suitability for that particular assignment
- Contracting for work that our organization is qualified to perform and assigning only qualified individuals to perform the work
- Upholding this Code and holding each other accountable to it

4.3 Duty of Fairness

Fairness involves representing ourselves in matters with consistency by evincing a commitment to impartiality, objectivity, openness, due process, and proportionality.

As practitioners in the global change management community we demonstrate duty of fairness by:

- Treating all people equitably based on merit and ability
- Dealing with each and every matter before us with consistency
- Demonstrating transparency in the decision-making process using appropriate criteria without undue favoritism or improper prejudice
- Conducting ourselves in a manner which is free from competing self-interest, prejudice, and favoritism
- Constantly reexamining our impartiality and objectivity, taking corrective action as appropriate
- Providing equal access to information to those who are authorized to have that information
- Making opportunities equally available to all qualified candidates
- Proactively and fully disclosing any real or potential conflicts of interest to the appropriate stakeholders
- Refraining from engaging in the decision-making process or otherwise attempting to influence outcomes when we realize that we have a real or potential conflict of interest, unless or until we have made full disclosure to the affected stakeholders, we have an approved mitigation plan, and we have obtained the consent of the stakeholders to proceed

Copyright © 2019 Association of Change Management Professionals® (ACMP®) All Rights Reserved

4.4 Duty of Respect

Respect is how we acknowledge and honor the absolute dignity of every person. As professionals we must continually show a high regard for ourselves, other people, reputation, the safety of others, and financial and other resources entrusted to us. An environment of respect engenders trust, confidence, and performance excellence by fostering mutual cooperation, which in turn supports an environment where diverse perspectives and views are encouraged and valued.

As practitioners in the global change management community we demonstrate duty of respect by:

- Informing ourselves about the norms and customs of others and avoid engaging in behaviors they might consider disrespectful
- Listening to others' points of view, and seeking to understand them
- Approaching directly those persons with whom we have a conflict or disagreement
- Conducting ourselves in a professional manner, even when it is not reciprocated
- Treating others with dignity and expect the same of our colleagues
- Acting with compassion and sensitivity to the feelings and needs of others
- Negotiating in good faith
- Refraining from using our expertise or position to influence the decisions or actions of others
- Refusing to act in an abusive manner toward others
- Respecting the property rights of others

4.5 Duty of Advancing the Discipline & Supporting Practitioners

Advancing the discipline and supporting practitioners to lead and practice ethical change management is at the core of the formation of ACMP. Through creating a community of professionals who share an ethos of consistently striving to deliver best practice and added value for their clients or employers, we advance the discipline of change management into a recognizable, respected profession.

As practitioners in the global change management community we demonstrate our collective ethos to advance the discipline by:

- Committing to share our knowledge, experience and tools to build consistency in value for clients or employers to the fullest extent possible without violating agreements of intellectual property rights with the clients or companies which the practitioner is associated
- Supporting practitioners through undertaking cutting edge research and sharing those findings
- Enabling ongoing education and accreditation within the framework of the Standards of ACMP for the profession
- Advocating for the profession by engaging in activities that enhance its credibility and value teaching at every opportunity – our clients, our peers, our employers and employees, and other practitioners and the global community

V. Adjudication and Appeals Process

The ACMP Board of Directors will appoint an Ethics Inquiry Task Force to review complaints and/or inquiries pursuant to procedures approved by the ACMP Board and made public. Ethical inquiries and or complaints will be submitted through the Ethics Inquiry form, reviewed and adjudicated through the Ethics Inquiry Task force, with findings/responses communicated to the complainant or inquirer and the ACMP Board of Directors. Violations of the ACMP Code of Ethics may result in sanctions by ACMP.

This reprint is for use with READY, Set, Change! Training
www.springboard-consult.com

www.acmpglobal.org

Made in the USA
Monee, IL
10 February 2025